T0010624

Made in
CHICAGO

Made in CHICAGO

STORIES BEHIND 30 GREAT HOMETOWN BITES

MONICA ENG and
DAVID HAMMOND

3 FIELDS BOOKS
An imprint of the University of Illinois Press
URBANA • CHICAGO • SPRINGFIELD

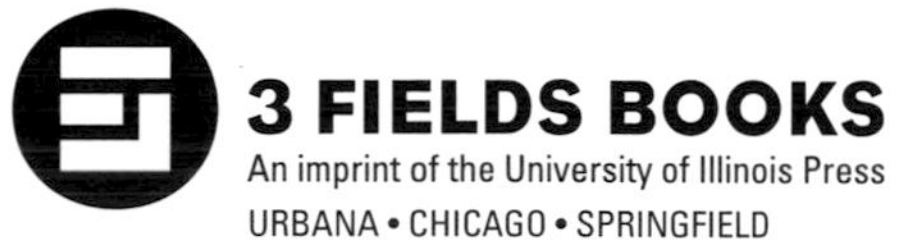

3 Fields Books is an imprint of the University of Illinois Press.

Manufactured in the United States of America
P 5 4 3 2
♾ This book is printed on acid-free paper.

Library of Congress Cataloging-in-Publication Data
Names: Eng, Monica, author. | Hammond, David (Resident of Chicago) author.
Title: Made in Chicago: stories behind 30 great hometown bites / Monica Eng and David Hammond.
Description: Urbana : 3 Fields Books, an imprint of University of Illinois Press, [2023] | Includes bibliographical references.
Identifiers: LCCN 2022034864 (print) | LCCN 2022034865 (ebook) | ISBN 9780252087059 (paperback) | ISBN 9780252054068 (ebook)
Subjects: LCSH: Cooking—Illinois—Chicago. | Restaurants—Illinois—Chicago—Guidebooks. | LCGFT: Cookbooks.
Classification: LCC TX715 .E5678 2023 (print) | LCC TX715 (ebook) | DDC 641.59773/11—dc23/eng/20220728
LC record available at https://lccn.loc.gov/2022034864
LC ebook record available at https://lccn.loc.gov/2022034865

To my mom, Ingrid, who taught me that there's always time to stop for the delicious things in life.

—Monica Eng

To my longtime traveling and dining companion, who also happens to be the best home cook I know, my wife, Carolyn Berg.

—David Hammond

CONTENTS

ACKNOWLEDGMENTS IX

INTRODUCTION 1

1 AKUTAGAWA 4

2 BIG BABY 9

3 BONE-IN PORK CHOP SANDWICH 13

4 BREADED STEAK SANDWICH 17

5 CHICKEN VESUVIO 22

6 CHICAGO CORN ROLL TAMALE 25

7 CHICAGO MIX 29

8 CHICAGO-STYLE EGG ROLL 33

9 CHICAGO HOT DOG 36

10 DEEP DISH PIZZA 42

11 FLAMING SAGANAKI 48

12 GIARDINIERA 52

13 GAM PONG CHICKEN WINGS 56

14 GYROS 60

15 ITALIAN BEEF SANDWICH 66

16 JIBARITO 70

17 JIM SHOE 74

18 MALÖRT 78

19 MAXWELL STREET POLISH 83

20 MILD SAUCE 87

21 MOTHER-IN-LAW 94

22 PEPPER AND EGG SANDWICH 98

23 PIZZA PUFF 101

24 RAINBOW CONE 105

25 RIB TIPS 110

26 SHRIMP DEJONGHE 114

27 STEAK AND LEMONADE 118

28 SWEET STEAK SUPREME SANDWICH 124

29 TAFFY GRAPES 129

30 TAVERN-STYLE PIZZA 132

REFERENCES 137

ACKNOWLEDGMENTS

We wish to acknowledge food historian Bruce Kraig, Professor Emeritus at Roosevelt University, for coming up with the idea for this book and for guiding us to some informative sources. Dr. Peter Engler provided invaluable insights about the foods of Chicago's South Side, and Gary Wiviott shared his considerable knowledge of barbecue history.

Many working people in the Chicago restaurant community shared their stories with us. The Yamauchi family, for instance, shared their family memories about Hamburger King, Chris Pacelli filled us in on the history of Al's #1 and Italian beef, and many others took the time to chat with us about the history of their unique food creations and the people who first served them. Many who are not named here gave generously of their time and expertise, and to them we are heavily indebted.

Monica Eng wishes to specifically thank her editors at the *Chicago Tribune* and WBEZ who, she says, "let me do so much background reporting for this over the years as part of my job."

David Hammond thanks his editors at *Newcity Chicago*, the *Chicago Sun-Times*, and the *Tribune*, as well as the *Wednesday Journal*. His most profound thanks go to the online food community at LTHForum.com, which he cofounded in the early 2000s, and which continues to be a primary source for anyone seeking to learn about street-level chow and fine dining in Chicago.

Made in
CHICAGO

INTRODUCTION

If you look hard enough, you can find a thousand stories simmered into every plate of food.

These are tales of long journeys, deep nostalgia, and fervent hopes. They're stories of dirt, water, seeds, plants, animals, farmers, truckers, millers, bakers, brewers, grocers, cooks, servers, and the many others who work hard to put food on our plates and into our bags of takeout.

The best of these stories are often about the innovators, folks who find themselves in a new place, with new materials, challenges, and customers to please. They're people who bring their own culinary history with them and use it to shape the ingredients they find at hand. In the process, they reimagine traditional foods and transform them into something new, fresh, even strange and provocative.

Some of these culinary creations become "local specialties" born of a need to create a food of one's own, something that reflects local tastes, of course, but is also a dish that other regions do not have. Regional foods are a unique voice of their place of origin, an expression of the people who live there, and for visitors, an entryway into the local culture.

Truth be told, sometimes these foods are not universally delicious or particularly replicable. But other times, lightning strikes: the new concoction really clicks and expands far beyond the individual kitchen where it originated to become part of the local culinary fabric—and sometimes, as is the case with the Chicago hot dog and deep dish pizza, even the national and international food pantheon.

These are the kinds of foods, people, and stories we've highlighted in these pages.

Some of the chapters that follow feature brand-new revelations unlikely to show up in any other guidebook. Others put a fresh spin on oft-told stories. But with all of them, we've aimed to scoop deeper into the research pot, to track down inventors, their kin, and well-informed purveyors. Sometimes these sources present tasty new details, and at other times they just serve up a side dish of their own stories to enhance the culinary record.

Still, every story we tell reflects the pride that local people feel for local foods, foods that may not be universally admired but ones that reflect the tastes and personalities of the folks who first prepared them and those who continue to enjoy them.

THE WHOLE CHICAGO SMORGASBORD

Looking at the whole smorgasbord of original Chicago foods can help sharpen common themes. One theme that clearly emerges is that we really like beef. This fondness for red meat might be a product of our meatpacking past or, as one interviewee suggested, a legacy of the first wave of fast-food entrepreneurs in Chicago, many of whom were Jewish. Dishes like tamales, sausages, frankfurters, gyros, and Pizza Puffs all underwent pork-to-beef makeovers before they marched into the Chicago fast-food hall of fame. And several other fast-food classics—Italian beef, sweet steaks, Jim Shoes, jibaritos, and breaded steak sandwiches—simply started and stayed beef-centric.

Another theme? Cross-cultural collision. Here the ingredients of one group—like cheese, sausage, and tomato sauce—get tucked into the ingredients of another, like a Mexican flour tortilla, and voilà, the Pizza Puff is born. These dishes pay tribute to culinary improvisors, Chicago's rich immigrant heritage, and a city that welcomes new chefs into our municipal kitchen with open arms . . . provided they feed us well.

So, what else do all these dishes say about a city that created and embraced them? It's clear that we have fiercely divided pizza preferences, a love for sweet and salty mixes, and, sadly, some entrenched culinary segregation. Good luck finding Southside creations like the Mother-in-Law or the sweet steak in North Side restaurants.

We hope that this book can break down some of those divides or at least get Chicagoans to try specialties on the opposite sides of town.

Skimming the table of contents, you might notice these classics don't exactly constitute a well-rounded diet, as they're many times a little heavy on the meat and carbs. In fact, the Chicago culinary canon screams that we're a hardy folk, people who've endured tough winters, know how to stretch a dime and how to use what's available to MacGyver ingredients into something special.

These dishes may not be particularly fancy, but they're creations that have endured and become part of the reason Chicago remains one of the premier food cities in the world.

USING THIS BOOK

We've written this book to serve everyone from the timid eater to the local food scholar, and from lifelong Chicagoans to visitors discovering the city for the very first time.

Our hope is that most readers will use this slim volume as a guidebook, one that can be kept in a glove compartment or bike satchel to serve as a companion around town. In each chapter, we've listed great spots to chow down on the dishes we've researched here. No doubt, some of the restaurants and street stands mentioned in this book will change over time, switch locations, or simply go out of business; that's the ephemeral, transitory nature of urban living. Whether the locations last or don't, the food they serve will at least provide guidance—and a kind of inspiration—to those who, after going through these pages, might pause in their reading to suddenly realize, "Hey, that sounds fantastic. I want to eat that!"

AKUTAGAWA

Monica Eng

HAMBURGER MEAT WITH CHOPPED ONIONS AND GREEN PEPPER, BEAN SPROUTS AND SCRAMBLED EGG, SERVED WITH A SIDE OF RICE AND GRAVY

Akutagawa at Rice 'N Bread. Photo: Monica Eng

In the middle of the twentieth century, Chicago's Wrigleyville was home to a huge working-class Japanese American community, the perfect place for the invention of the Akutagawa.

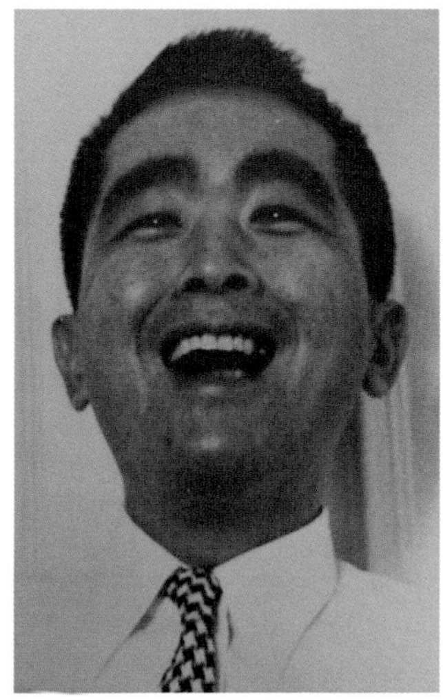

Tom Yamauchi made the Akutagawa for a friend, and then for other customers who wanted it
Photo: Courtesy of Barb Satoh

A blend of standard American diner ingredients with a few Asian touches, the Akutagawa embodies the tension between being Japanese and "American" in a post–World War II United States. At that time, Japanese Americans, who had been released from internment camps and forcibly relocated to Chicago, were told they needed to shed their Japanese-ness for their own good. Documents show that during exit interviews from the camps, they were asked things like "Will you try to develop such American habits that will cause you to be accepted readily into American social groups?"

Barbara Satoh's mother was among the twenty thousand Japanese Americans who relocated to Chicago after the war.

"She moved here after being interned in Gila, Arizona," Satoh recalled.

But her dad, Tom Yamauchi, was born into one of the few Japanese American families that were already in Chicago. Satoh said her father served in the U.S. military during World War II.

"He had been in training to be an interpreter, so they could interview Japanese prisoners," she said. "But after the war, he started working as a cook for his father-in-law at a diner downtown called the Delaware Garden."

By 1954 Yamauchi had saved enough money to open his own place in Wrigleyville, just down the street from the Chicago Cubs' ballpark: an American-style diner called Hamburger King.

"It was just a nine-stool little place on a triangle of land at Clark and Sheffield," Satoh said. "The neighborhood was very working class at the time, but [our restaurant] was affordable. So, it became the home away from home for lots of people in the neighborhood. It became like their kitchen."

Here Tom Yamauchi served, yes, the namesake hamburger with crisp golden fries, but also chili, soups, and daily specials like meatloaf, ribs and sauerkraut, and stuffed peppers. There were also a few subtle Asian touches, "like vinegar cucumber pickles and rice—always rice with everything," Satoh said. "Also, there was this dish where he chopped up a pork chop and seared it on the grill with green pepper, onions and teriyaki sauce."

An early standout at the diner was its famous bowl of rice and gravy—a perfect rib-sticking meal for the budget diner.

"It went for a quarter for a small bowl and seventy-five cents for a large ramen bowl," Satoh said. "It kind of warmed your tummy, and people would come in just for that."

Satoh recalls the Hamburger King clientele as a multicultural parade of shift workers, Chicago Cubs organization staffers, baseball players, police on the beat, Japanese Americans (many by way of Hawaii), and working-class families from the neighborhood.

By 1968, Yamauchi was able to move the business across Sheffield Avenue to a little storefront spot with a counter and room for actual tables. It was just two doors down from a classic Japanese American hangout, the Nisei Lounge, which remains Wrigleyville's oldest bar. "The Nisei Lounge didn't serve food and we didn't have a lot of seats, so sometimes the overflow would go to the bar, and we'd serve them there through a door in the back that connected the two places," Satoh said. "My mother didn't like that we were high school and college students serving people at a bar where they were drinking beer. It was probably illegal, but there we were, taking orders and carrying food and dirty dishes back and forth. Years later, new owners said they'd heard a rumor that there used to be a door that went through the barber shop and connected to the bar. We told them it had all been boarded up."

It was here in the late 1960s that the Akutagawa was born.

ORIGINS OF THE AKUTAGAWA

"Every morning my dad would get up at four because we opened at 6:00 a.m.," Satoh recalled. "He liked these hours because it meant he got off at two, which allowed him to go next door to Nisei Lounge, have a beer, and watch the Cubs on game days. And if one of us was working, we'd be responsible for driving him home."

Hamburger King was a regular haunt for Chicago Cubs managers and coaches in the 1970s. Satoh remembers them gathering there on summer mornings to eat, drink coffee, and read the sports sections.

"They had cigars in their mouths, and they read a stack of papers to see what the columnists had to say about them, good or bad," she said.

Another frequent diner was a guy named George Akutagawa. He had a broad face, gregarious personality, and a big smile. He liked to drink and watch Cubs games at the Nisei. But when he got hungry, he'd toddle down to the Hamburger King.

"George was a regular and good friend of my father," explained Satoh's sister Emmie Yamauchi, who worked at the restaurant as a server in her teens. "Like a lot of the Japanese people in the area, he was from Hawaii, which is why we served so much Spam."

"I am not sure what George's job was," Satoh said, "but we remember that he wore a suit and tie to work."

When George Akutagawa took his seat at Hamburger King one day, Satoh said, he asked his pal Tom Yamauchi to make him something special. The dish he dreamed up used ingredients Yamauchi used a lot already—along with bean sprouts—in a preparation that was not entirely different from, say, Japanese okonomiyaki or loco moco, the latter a dish popular in George Akutagawa's Hawaii.

"It was made with hamburger meat, chopped onions and green pepper, bean sprouts and scrambled egg," Satoh recalled.

And, of course, Yamauchi served it to his friend with a side of rice.

"After a while people saw what George was eating, and they said 'Hey, that looks pretty good. I'd like to have some of that too'," Satoh recalled. "So, my dad made it for them and after a while we just started calling it the Akutagawa.

"People liked it because it was pretty hearty and nutritious, especially if you took out the meat, so it could be vegetarian. Some people thought it was supposed to be like okonomiyaki, but it was more like egg foo young. It was only called the Akutagawa during the day," she added. "At night, it became the 'Hamburger Royale,' without the minced onions and with more big pieces of vegetables."

Over the decades, the Akutagawa remained a specialty only at Hamburger King. But in later years it made forays into other neighborhoods. It was featured on the menu at the now defunct North Shore Grill in Edgewater, where a former Hamburger King cook served it with tofu and a side of rice and gravy.

Still, "he spelled it on the menu more like Octogawa, like it had eight ingredients or something," Satoh said of the North Shore Grill version. "But eight had nothing to do with it."

Satoh says one woman even told her that the Akutagawa became part of her childhood family home breakfasts.

"She said her mother had to learn how to make it because her father loved it so much," Satoh said. "I couldn't believe it."

Today you can still order it as a secret off-the-menu item at the Fullerton Restaurant in Logan Square, as well as at the restaurant that replaced Hamburger King.

So, was the Akutagawa a subversive attempt to recreate a Japanese dish at a time when Japanese Americans were told to tone down their Japanese-ness? Or was it just a quirky way to please a friend and customer? That answer may be lost to time, as both George Akutagawa (who moved back to Hawaii) and Tom Yamauchi have passed away.

But their memory lives on in a dish that customers still order dozens of times a week—along with a side of rice and gravy—in the old Hamburger King dining room in Wrigleyville.

The place has changed hands a few times since Yamauchi sold it in 1980. Sonia Hwang ran it for several years and added some homestyle Korean touches to the menu. But the latest proprietors, who bought it in 2013, made the biggest changes. They remodeled the room, added more Korean dishes, and renamed the restaurant Rice'N Bread.

WHERE TO GET AKUTAGAWA

Rice'N Bread
3435 N. Sheffield Ave.
773-985-5848

Fullerton Restaurant
2400 W. Fullerton Ave.
773-384-5500

PREPARING AKUTAGAWA AT HOME (RECIPE FROM BARB SATOH)

Serves 1

Ingredients

⅛ to ¼ pound ground beef shaped into a hamburger patty
⅛ cup minced green pepper
⅛ cup minced onion
½ cup bean sprouts or other vegetables (can be adjusted to taste)
2 eggs, beaten well in a small bowl
Salt and pepper to taste

Procedure

1. Preheat skillet on medium high.
2. Put hamburger patty in skillet and place green peppers and onions on top of the patty.
3. Let hamburger patty cook until seared.
4. Lower heat to medium.
5. Carefully turn the patty over so that green peppers and onions will cook under it.
6. Cook for 5-7 minutes or until green peppers and onions are tender.
7. Use a spatula to "cut up" the patty, green peppers, and onions until the patty is in small (not tiny) pieces.
8. Add bean sprouts and continue to cook until sprouts are tender but not mushy.
9. Pour the 2 eggs onto the meat/vegetable mixture. Let eggs cook for a minute, then begin turning and mixing with the spatula until cooked through. Do not overmix it.
10. Salt and pepper to taste.

Serve with a side of rice and gravy.

BIG BABY

Monica Eng

DOUBLE CHEESEBURGER WITH GRILLED ONIONS ON TOP, CHEESE BETWEEN THE TWO PATTIES, AND PICKLE COINS, MUSTARD, AND KETCHUP UNDERNEATH THE BOTTOM PATTY

A classic Big Baby. Photo: Monica Eng

The Big Baby might strike you as kind of a nothing burger—or, at most, just a plain old double cheeseburger. After all, it consists of two all-beef patties, mustard, ketchup, cheese, and grilled onions on a sesame seed bun—strongly reminiscent of a nationally famous burger with a bigger name. But when a Big Baby is done just right, this Chicago creation sings with perfectly balanced flavor, beautiful texture, and an understated genius.

Plus, it's got a great back story, one shaped by immigration, a french fry salesperson, and some antiquated workplace behavior.

THE ORIGIN STORY

So now that we know its ingredients, how was this baby born and who gave it a name?

That's what I tried to answer as the Curious City reporter for WBEZ, Chicago Public Radio. The actual question was about why there were so many seemingly unconnected places called "Nicky's" that served the Big Baby or something just like it.

My journey to find an answer took me down some blind alleys where I was sold some false—if tasty—burger theories before eventually finding the man who started it all.

WHERE WAS THE BIG BABY BORN?

Given all the Big Babies served up on the Southwest Side, I figured that would be a fertile place to start my search. First stop was a joint my friend Louisa Chu recommended called Nicky's the Real McCoy, on South Kedzie Avenue near 58th Street. The owners operated three Nicky's locations, but this was the oldest, bearing a sign that proudly proclaimed, "Chicago's Original Est. 1969."

Here, I munched on a delicious Big Baby while manager Manoli Marneris regaled me with a great story about the origin of the burger. He said his dad Jimmy thought up the creation and named it as a tribute to his grandfather, Nicky Marneris.

"It was 1968 when my father wanted to open up some kind of burger joint, but he knew he had to have something that could compete with the Big Mac," Marneris said, pointing at a big McDonald's franchise across the street.

"So, his response to that was the Big Baby, which is just like the Big Mac except for the grilled onions—and those grilled onions kept it very juicy no matter what. So even if it had to travel a long distance, it was always that same tasty burger, and it kept the same consistent flavor every time."

This all seemed very convincing, and I ate up the story—along with a few burgers—before heading back to the office to finish writing my article. But just days before the story was to be released, I got a surprise.

My editor Jessica Pupovac and I were out sampling Big Babies on the Southwest Side for a recommendation list when something slapped us in the face like a big bag of frozen beef patties. It was four words emblazoned on a sign outside a Nicky's at 6142 South Archer Avenue: "The Original Since 1967."

Wait, 1967? That was two years before Nicky's the Real McCoy opened on Kedzie. How could this be? Had I fallen for a hamburger hoax?

We sidled up to the counter inside, asked for a couple of burgers, and then started asking questions. Owner Angelo Lilas was only too happy to answer.

"*This* is the original Nicky's, and this is the original Big Baby," he said, adding the caveat that there had been one older Nicky's restaurant in south suburban Summit, Illinois, starting in 1962, but it was now gone.

So, who started the Nicky's and invented the Big Baby?

Lilas said it was a man named Nicky who sold this location to his father, Jim Lilas.

Side note: I should mention that all the Nicky's owners I've mentioned so far are Greek Americans, an ethnic group heavily engaged in "American-style" food service—from confectionaries and ice cream shops to diners and burger joints—for much of the twentieth century in Chicago and the United States.

Angelo Lilas said the original Nicky was also Greek, but he couldn't recall Nicky's last name. He only knew that Nicky was "retired and was a pretty private guy. So, I don't think he'll want to talk."

Angelo did, however, put us in touch with his dad, Jim, who offered confirmation that the Nicky's on Archer was indeed the oldest remaining Big Baby–teria in Chicago.

"And I have the papers to prove it," he noted.

On top of that, the elder Lilas presented two more things: an offer to reach out to the Big Baby founder (who was a fellow parishioner at his church) and the revelation of Nicky's full name.

"His name is Nick, Nicky Vagenas, and if I see him at church, I will tell him to call you."

While we were waiting for Lilas to set up a meeting, we worked our end of the investigation by calling every Vagenas in the book. We even unsuccessfully staked out his suburban church one Sunday to see if we could find him.

And then we gave up.

Weeks later, though, we got a voicemail at work from an elderly man who claimed to be *the* Nicky Vagenas of Big Baby fame.

Jessica and I scrambled into a recording booth, called the number back, and asked the octogenarian every question we could think of.

Did you really create the Big Baby to compete with the Big Mac?

"No, no, no, no, no, no, no, no, no!" he insisted emphatically.

So then how did you come up with it?

"I don't know. It just came to me," Vagenas said cheerfully. "I tried everything and the grilled onions on a double cheeseburger—well, people liked it and it went on, and that's it."

So how did he land upon the name Big Baby? Vagenas explained that it came from a female employee who worked with him at the Nicky's on Archer.

"I was working with a woman side by side," he said. "And I said, 'Hi, big baby,' and she said, 'Why don't you call that double cheeseburger Big Baby?'"

And so, he did. But Vagenas claims he can't quite remember the female employee's name.

He explains he got into the burger business in the mid-1960s after running an unsuccessful traditional diner (also called Nicky's) in Summit that "wasn't making a lot of money."

His inspiration to shift gears came from a tip he got from his french fry supplier.

"I asked him where he sold a lot of fries, and he said, 'I sell a lot of fries at [a fast-food stand] at Laramie and 22nd Street.' So, I went to look at the hot dog stand over there and I saw all this business," he recalled. "And the next week, I went to look for a hot dog stand."

Once Vagenas opened his first Nicky's fast-food stand on Archer in 1967, he quickly got the hang of the business model and went on to open nine more locations.

"I opened them, and then after a year or two I sold them," he said, noting the buyers were almost always fellow Greek immigrants whose employees and relatives often left to open offshoots.

One of those Greek immigrants was Manoli Marneris's father. Vagenas says he wasn't the person who invented the burger, but he also doesn't hold a grudge.

"I give them a lot of credit if they work hard and make a lot of money," he said.

Born in 1934, Vagenas still seemed to be enjoying the life he built on fast-food stands. So how did he explain being so active and healthy after a life of burgers?

"I go to sleep at night, and I don't think about bad things," he says. "I don't owe anybody any money and they don't owe me any money. So, I sleep like a baby."

INGREDIENTS

As noted above, the components of a Big Baby bear a strong resemblance to those of the McDonald's Big Mac—just without the lettuce, special sauce, or extra layer of bun. This has led some folks to insist the two big burgers are linked—despite Vagenas's claim otherwise.

For many, the appeal of the burger is not so much in its ingredients as the way it's stacked, using a sequence designed to maximize eating pleasure. From top to bottom, the Big Baby goes like this: top bun, grilled onions, burger patty, American cheese, second patty, three pickle coins, mustard, ketchup, and bottom bun.

The sequence creates a soft, fatty richness at the top of the sandwich with its tender bun, caramelized onions, melty cheese, and meat. They're kind of like the bass notes of a masterful concerto.

Meanwhile, the bottom of the sandwich is designed to deliver sharp, acidic notes of mustard, ketchup, and a few crunchy pickle coins. Call these the squeaky treble notes that balance things out.

If you're really lucky, there will be one more flourish—a griddle-toasted bun that brings a final buttery crispness to this Southwest Side work of art.

WHERE TO GET BIG BABIES

Nicky's Hot Dogs
6142 S. Archer Ave.
773-585-3675

Nicky's The Real McCoy
5801 S. Kedzie Ave.
773-436-6458

Jacky's Hot Dogs
5415 S. Pulaski Rd.
773-767-7676

BONE-IN PORK CHOP SANDWICH

David Hammond

GRIDDLED PORK CHOP ON A BUN, BONE-IN, WITH ONIONS AND MUSTARD (SPORT PEPPERS OPTIONAL)

Bone-in pork chop sandwich. Photo: David Hammond

It's a sandwich that's almost too easy to prepare: the bone-in pork chop is griddled and dropped on a bun, squirted with a swirl of mustard, loaded with cooked onions, maybe some sport peppers, and boom, that's it.

Though a seemingly low-effort production, the pork chop sandwich is delicious, and it is a quintessential workingman's food.

The first documented serving of the bone-in pork chop sandwich was at Jim's Original, a street-side stand that has operated in the Maxwell Street area since the middle of the last century.

EAT WITH CARE

Many Chicago chefs would concur that meats cooked with the bone in (including a bone-in ribeye or a slab of ribs) are more delicious than they would be if the bone had been removed prior to cooking. This theory lacks some quantifiable proof, though it's likely that the bone does serve to insulate the meat so that moisture is better maintained even when the bone-in cut of meat is subjected to a hot metal griddle.

There is nothing dainty about eating a bone-in pork chop sandwich. There is, however, a trick to it. "You have to know where the bone is before you take your first bite," cautions Jim Christopoulos, the current owner of Jim's Original and the grandson of James "Jimmy" Stefanovich, who opened his first food stand at the corner of Halsted and Maxwell at the old Maxwell Street Market, Chicago's storied open-air peddlers' market.

Our suggestion: when you unwrap your sandwich, hold the bone in the bun with one hand and eat from the other end, taking care not to chomp down on the bone. Because you're holding onto the bone, you always know where it is, so there's less chance you'll bite into it.

Eating this sandwich is a mess. You end up with little shreds of grease-soaked bun in your hand. Many pull the bare bone out of the bun and gnaw on it; it's not unusual to see grown people standing around Jim's, sucking on pork bones like kids gnawing popsicles.

Because eating the pork chop sandwich requires some dexterity and care, keep in mind that many places that sell the pork chop sandwich don't have any seating. However, you may not want to eat this sandwich walking along or even standing on the sidewalk (although if you're at Jim's, you'll see a lot of people doing just that). Instead, as it's likely you drove to Jim's, you can perch yourself on a front or back bumper or use the car roof or trunk as a table (what we in Chicago call "dining al trunko"). This way, you'll be able to better focus on what you're doing, which is a good thing if you don't have comprehensive dental insurance.

MAXWELL STREET: HOTBED OF CULINARY INNOVATION

At Jim's Original today (which is no longer located on Maxwell Street, though it is nearby the original location), you get a thick pork chop, about seven ounces. "We will make a double pork chop sandwich, but it's an off-menu item" says Christopoulos. "Twenty-five years ago, I would have taken the double. I loved the double."

Though the standard sandwich at Jim's includes just the one big chop, it's very juicy, owing in part to the brining prior to cooking, but also to the bone itself. "I'm going to keep cooking it with the bone, because that's how it always was, but also because everything with the bone in, it tastes better," says Christopoulos. "It's always moister and juicier right close by the bone."

The surest way to ensure juiciness is to use a thicker chop, and Jim's does.

As with the Maxwell Street Polish (chapter 19), the other original Chicago food born at Jim's, the proximity of the original Maxwell Street Market to the Union Stockyards to the south played a role in the development of this menu item. "We were close to the slaughterhouses, and pork was an easy thing to get," says Christopoulos, and in the days before modern transportation systems, being a few miles from the source of meat made a huge difference to early vendors of sausage and other meat products.

At Jim's, they cut their own porkchops. "We've got a bone saw," says Christopoulos, "and we get the whole pork back. It used to come in fresh, but now it's frozen and everything is more industrialized. The pigs are raised in clean houses, and the meat is flash frozen, which means it might lose some of its tenderness and flavor; that's why we now brine it in salt, pepper, water, and a little oil."

SPORT PEPPERS, A CLASSIC CONDIMENT

One of the signature condiments on this sandwich, the sport pepper, though it seems to have originated in the southern United States, is frequently offered on fully dressed Chicago hot dogs (chapter 9), the Maxwell Street Polish (chapter 19), and the bone-in pork chop sandwich. Whatever you're ordering, even if you say you want "everything" on it, the man at the counter will frequently double-check, asking, "Sport peppers, too?" I guess they see a lot of these peppers getting tossed into the trash, so they want to make sure you really want them. Pro tip: unless you're a heat-seeking chili head, if you're ordering a bone-in pork chop sandwich or Maxwell Street Polish and you ask for sport peppers, gingerly take a small bite of one before chomping into it. These can be some high-impact chili peppers, and a bite of one early on can numb your tongue for the rest of the meal.

The word "sport" is used to describe several different types of peppers. The sport pepper one finds on a bone-in pork chop sandwich is frequently a type of yellowish-green serrano or tabasco chili pepper. With up to twenty thousand or so Scoville units of heat, it's a rare street food enthusiast who can down a whole one.

At Jim's, they use serrano peppers, which they pickle onsite. Christopoulos explains, "We use water, vinegar, salt, sugar, and proprietary spices. Then we let the pickles rest in the pickling solution for approximately two weeks."

These made-in-house sport peppers add an artisanal touch to such a simple sandwich.

In a twenty-first-century line extension, Christopoulos told us he just launched a "pepper-hot mustard," which is Plochman's mustard mixed with sport peppers;

you can have it on sandwiches or buy bottles of the condiment to take home. This combination makes some sense because on sandwiches with mustard, you're likely to also find sport peppers. So why not combine the two? "And because the peppers are all chopped up," says Christopoulos, "you can get them in a more measured dose," which will immediately make sense to any one of us who has ever chomped into a whole sport pepper only to descend immediately into regret.

WHERE TO GET A BONE-IN PORK CHOP SANDWICH

Jim's Original
1250 S. Union Ave.
312-733-7820

Express Grill
1260 S. Union Ave.
312-738-2112

The Original Maxwell Street
3801 W. Harrison St.
773-940-2270

HOW TO PREPARE A BONE-IN PORK CHOP SANDWICH AT HOME

Serves 6

Ingredients

6 hamburger buns
6 thin pork chops
1 gallon water
1 cup salt
1 teaspoon pepper
1 cup sugar
½ cup corn oil for brine; 2–4 tablespoons corn oil for cooking onions and pork chops
2 large yellow onions, sliced thin
Mustard
Sport peppers

Procedure

1. Prepare brine with water, salt, pepper, sugar, and ½ cup corn oil; place pork chops in brine and leave brining for about 6 hours.
2. In frying pan, add 1–2 tablespoons corn oil and lightly sauté onions over low-to-medium heat until limp (about 20 minutes); set onions aside.
3. In same frying pan, add 1–2 tablespoons of corn oil and cook chops over medium-to-high heat. Flip as necessary until browned on both sides.
4. Remove chops from heat, nestle onto buns, and top with onions, mustard, and sport peppers.

BREADED STEAK SANDWICH

David Hammond

POUNDED STEAK, BREADED, FRIED, DRENCHED IN RED GRAVY, LAID INTO GONNELLA BREAD, AND SPRINKLED WITH MOZZARELLA, SWEET PEPPERS OR GIARDINIERA, OR BOTH

Breaded steak sandwich. Photo: David Hammond

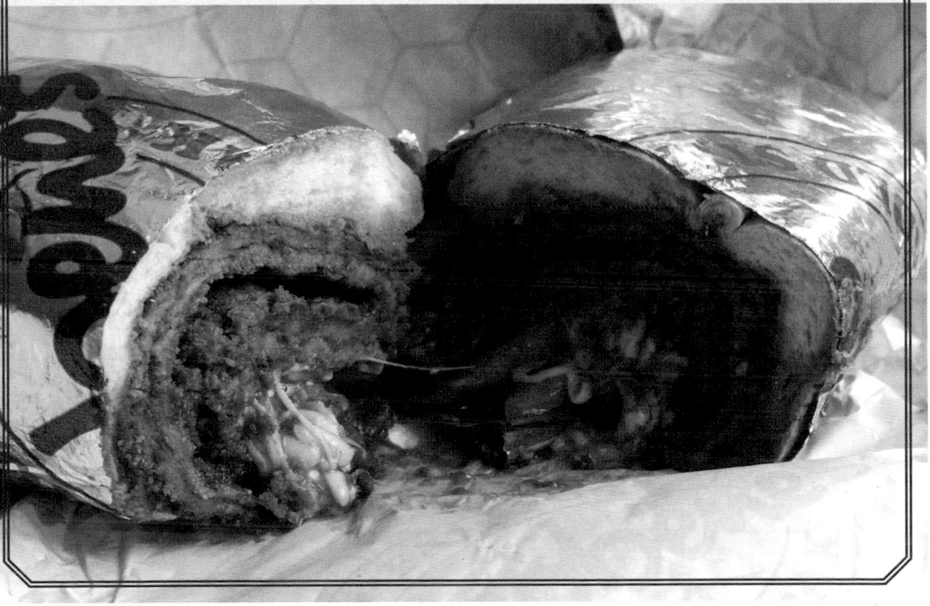

When we arrived at Ricobene's in Armour Square for lunch one summer afternoon, we saw police cars in the big lot across the street and a fire department vehicle standing in front with the motor running. A police officer, a few sandwiches in his hands, held the door for us as we walked in. Tables were filled with all kinds of people, lots of municipal workers, several groups of construction workers wearing their yellow vests, guys in suits, and tables of moms with kids. Ricobene's is a restaurant for everyone, but especially for people who work hard and, when the lunch bell rings, are ready for a belly full of food. And you'll need a good-sized appetite to finish even the "regular" breaded steak sandwich at Ricobene's.

Ricobene's is one of Chicago's best-known sources for the breaded steak sandwich, which is in many ways simply a chicken-fried steak with marinara sauce, rather than white gravy, and melted mozzarella, served on a segment of bread from the iconic Gonnella bakery. The standard condiments, as with the Italian beef sandwich (chapter 15), are sweet peppers, giardiniera (chapter 12), or both; we usually go with both, as this combination provides a good blast of sweet and heat, both of which complement the meat.

After eating a breaded steak sandwich from Ricobene's, a friend of mine once reflected, "There were moments when I was absolutely convinced that I was eating breaded carpet padding." There are clearly those who love this sandwich and those who do not. The breaded steak sandwich is a prime example of how we Americans will make a sandwich out of anything.

According to a 2015 article in *USA Today*, "The breaded steak sandwich from Ricobene's in Chicago is the best sandwich in the world." This claim is impossible to prove, of course, but it does reflect the passion of many for this sandwich, another Chicago original from the city's Italian American community.

IN THE PROUD TRADITION OF THE MILANESA AND THE WIENER SCHNITZEL

Sam Ricobene Jr., the son of Sam Ricobene Sr., who is generally credited with creating the breaded steak sandwich, said his grandparents, Rosario and Antonia, ran a pushcart business in 1946. They started by selling vegetables, but at one point they began selling hot meatball and sausage sandwiches. It wasn't until 1976 that Rosario and his sons—Sam, Frank, and Russell—started their own version of the breaded steak sandwich. "My dad was the creative mind behind a lot of the food," Sam said. "This is what he came up with."

According to a 2012 article in the *Chicago Tribune*, Ricobene's founder, Sam Ricobene Sr., "may not have invented the breaded steak sandwich that headlines the menu of his family's restaurants, but he perfected it. And the other places that might have claimed the title of originator are long gone, according to Mr. Ricobene's son, Sam Jr. 'There are still arguments in the neighborhood over who did it first,' said the younger Ricobene [Sam Jr.], 'but [Sam Ricobene Sr.] did it right.'"

On Ricobene's menu, under "Famous Breaded Steak Sandwiches," the first item listed is the "'Original' KING SIZE Breaded Steak." The quotation marks around "original" may lead one to assume that Ricobene's was maybe not the first to serve this sandwich, but no one else has stepped up so boldly to claim that distinction, and of all the places serving this sandwich, Ricobene's seems the most widely known.

Though tracing origins can be a tricky business, Ricobene's website states that the restaurant has been preparing the breaded steak sandwich since 1946.

It might be correct to say that the classic Italian Milanesa, served all over the world—including Italy, of course, but also Mexico, Argentina, and Uruguay—is the forerunner of Ricobene's breaded steak sandwich. Another forerunner would be wiener schnitzel, which is also a piece of meat, traditionally veal, that's been pounded, breaded, and fried.

The wiener schnitzel, unlike the breaded steak sandwich, is usually served on a plate and eaten with a knife and fork. The breaded steak sandwich, on the other hand, is drenched in tomato sauce and served on a roll. The day we visited Ricobene's, I was the only person in the place eating the sandwich with a knife and fork and, yes, I felt like a fancy lad.

THE FREDDY, COUSIN TO THE BREADED STEAK SANDWICH

On another branch of the same evolutionary tree as the breaded steak sandwich is the Freddy, a sandwich of oblong sausage patties, covered in red sauce and melted mozzarella, dressed with sautéed green peppers.

Dr. Peter Engler, writing in LTHForum.com, the Chicago-based culinary chat site, notes: "The Freddy's birthplace and natural habitat is the far Southwest Side, around Beverly, Evergreen Park and Blue Island. It originated in the early 1970s and as businesses split or were sold, the sandwich moved on but also stayed at its original home . . . Benito [Benny] Russo is generally acknowledged as the father of the Freddy (as well as the father of Freddy, after whom the sandwich was named). While Benny was at Chuck's Pizza in Beverly in the early 1970s, he put together the sandwich (obviously not an original creation) and named it after his son."

BEST SANDWICH IN THE WORLD?

The breaded steak sandwich is delicious. The meat is tender but with good texture, the sauce mild and slightly sweet, a perfect foil for hot giardiniera (chapter 12). Amazingly, even the "original" king size breaded steak sandwich holds together, due to the gluey mozzarella and the bread, which demonstrates truly remarkable tensile strength, and retains its integrity despite being wrapped around a wet mass of meat, sauce, and condiments. Even the small sandwich is a hefty handful.

Is it the best sandwich in the world? Who knows, but looking around the Ricobene's dining room one afternoon, we see the breaded steak sandwich at almost every table. At those tables, diners slam the gigantic two-fisted creation into their pieholes while big globs of sauce and cheese stream onto plates, faces, and laps.

There seem to be not enough napkins in Chicago to wipe the mouth of all the saucy cheese. The sandwich is kind of a monstrosity. Eating it isn't easy, but the struggle is way worth it.

Even in Chicago, however, the breaded steak sandwich from Ricobene's tends not to get the credit it deserves. Ted Berg, the *USA Today* writer who dubbed this sandwich "the best in the world," bemoaned the fact that it ranked dead last in a *Chicago Magazine* listing of the twelve best sandwiches in Chicago. "I find it difficult," Berg wrote, "to believe there are 11 other perfect sandwiches in one city. And I can attest, as a reviewer of sandwiches, that interesting and particularly photogenic sandwiches often receive undue praise because of the way they make the sandwich reviewer's job easier and are not necessarily rewarded for deliciousness alone."

The Ricobene's breaded steak sandwich was first conceived years before Instagram. There's no denying, however, that it's far from a handsome handful. So just close your eyes, take a bite, and see if you like the way it tastes. If you do, you should just keep your eyes closed all through lunch. Ricobene's breaded steak sandwich is not pretty, but it is tasty.

WHERE TO GET A BREADED STEAK SANDWICH

Fabulous Freddie's Italian Eatery
701 W. 31st St.
312-808-0147

Nonna Soluri's Italian Deli
3142 S. Morgan St.
773-247-8777

Ricobene's
252 W. 26th St.
312-225-5555

HOW TO PREPARE A BREADED STEAK SANDWICH AT HOME

Serves 4

Ingredients

4 thin sirloin steaks, ¼ pound each

1 egg, beaten

1½ cups breadcrumbs

2 tablespoons canola oil

4 hamburger buns

2 cups marinara sauce (can use one of the many premade sauces in jars)

1 cup mozzarella, shredded

Procedure

1. Pound each steak as thin as possible; it's best to use a meat mallet, but if you don't have that kitchen tool, you can use a rolling pin.
2. Dip each steak in the beaten egg, then dredge in breadcrumbs; repeat for a thicker breading.
3. Fry the steaks in the canola oil, about 3 minutes on each side.
4. Place each steak on a hamburger bun, ladle on the marinara sauce, and sprinkle with mozzarella.

5

CHICKEN VESUVIO

David Hammond

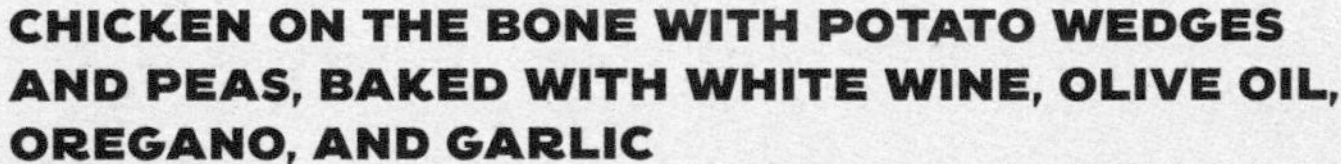

CHICKEN ON THE BONE WITH POTATO WEDGES AND PEAS, BAKED WITH WHITE WINE, OLIVE OIL, OREGANO, AND GARLIC

Homemade chicken Vesuvio. Photo: David Hammond

Sitting down to a steaming plate of chicken Vesuvio during the colder months, it'd be hard to imagine a more suitable dinner: the bone-in chicken and the crisp potatoes are hearty and satisfying, with the peas suggesting the green of springtime during what sometimes seems the endless snow of a Chicago winter.

Chicken Vesuvio suggests Mount Vesuvius, the volcano that destroyed Pompeii with a shower of fire and ash. Chicken Vesuvio must be spicy hot, right? Wrong. There is no hint of heat in the traditional chicken Vesuvio, which, it's generally accepted, was not named after the volcano but after Chicago's now long-gone Vesuvio Restaurant, once located at 15 East Wacker Drive.

Chicken Vesuvio may be the most popular of all Chicago original dishes, found on menus across the country and even around the world. But did chicken Vesuvio originate in the restaurant after which it is named?

Maybe . . . but maybe not.

According to food writer and linguist Dr. Anthony Buccini, the origins may be much humbler.

"At the risk," wrote Buccini, "of being attacked for a lack of appreciation for Chicago's place in culinary history, I fail to grasp the basis of the claim that 'Vesuvio' chicken was in any meaningful sense invented in Chicago. There are a number of variants that can be legitimately called 'Chicken Vesuvio,' and the kinds of variation allowed place the dish squarely amidst a continuum of southern Italian roasted chicken preparations."

What seems beyond doubt is that this dish was popularized by the folks at Vesuvio Restaurant, who put chicken Vesuvio on their menu sometime in the 1930s.

CONTENDERS FOR THE TITLE OF CHICKEN VESUVIO'S ORIGINATOR

Italian Village, Chicago's oldest Italian restaurant, also claims to be the birthplace of chicken Vesuvio. According to my email correspondence with owner Gina Capitanini, "The information is rather vague as to if my grandfather invented chicken Vesuvio. I was told it's a dish that he brought over from Italy, and when he opened his restaurant in 1927, he put it on his menu. Our chicken Vesuvio never had peas on it and many other restaurants use peas. The name Vesuvio stems from this dish being so flavorful it bursts in your mouth."

At Italian Village, chef Jose Torres follows a traditional recipe, including cut-up chicken, olive oil, white wine, salt, pepper, garlic, oregano, and canola oil (this last ingredient is a slight variation on the traditional recipe, which used olive rather than canola oil). The quick pan-frying of the chicken is a critical step, Torres tells me in a telephone interview, adding, "You want to get the oil hot before you put the chicken in, skin side down, then you flip it over to the bone side to get a nice crispiness all around.

"This is how we've done it for years," says Torres. "It's tradition. It brings in a lot of flavor to sauté the chicken with herbs, and it looks more appetizing and appealing. When you stack it up, it looks more like a volcano, Mount Vesuvius!"

The potatoes can be browned in the same pan as the chicken, and then everything is baked together, except the peas, which (if you're using them), go on at the end.

It's important to cook the chicken on the bone because, as Torres says, "The bone keeps it juicy and moist," though it can be prepared "without the bone, for people who don't want to mess with the bone, or skinless, for those who don't want the fat or calories in the skin."

WHERE TO GET CHICKEN VESUVIO

Harry Caray's Italian Steakhouse
33 W. Kinzie St.
312-828-0966

Gene & Georgetti
500 N. Franklin St.
312-527-3718

The Village
71 W. Monroe St.
312-332-7005

HOW TO PREPARE CHICKEN VESUVIO AT HOME

Ingredients

3 pounds bone-in, skin-on chicken pieces
Salt and pepper
2 tablespoons dried oregano
2 teaspoons garlic
¾ cup olive oil
4 russets or 6 red potatoes, cut into wedges
10–12 whole garlic cloves, peeled
1½ cups white wine
1½ cups chicken broth
1 cup frozen peas

Procedure

1. Season chicken with salt, pepper, oregano, and garlic.
2. Warm olive oil in a large, heavy skillet; brown seasoned chicken pieces and potato wedges, then remove from skillet and place in a roasting pan.
3. Add garlic cloves and cook until golden.
4. Deglaze pan with wine and add chicken broth; cook down and pour over chicken and potatoes.
5. Bake at 350 degrees Fahrenheit for about 90 minutes; add peas after 75 minutes or so.

CHICAGO CORN ROLL TAMALE

David Hammond

CORN MEAL SHAPED INTO A TUBE WITH A CORE OF LIGHTLY SEASONED MEAT, SOLD IN PAPER OR PLASTIC WRAPPERS

Chicago corn roll tamale. Photo: Supreme Tamale Company

Growing up in the 1950s in Chicago's Northwest Side neighborhood of Portage Park, we'd collect nickels and dimes by returning for refunds the soda and beer bottles we'd scavenged from construction sites. Our earnings were frequently deployed at a food vendor who did business from a small white trailer at the southwest corner of Central and Montrose. The grizzled old-timer at the takeout window had a limited menu, but he always had Chicago corn roll tamales, usually the least expensive item on the menu.

The tamales we bought as kids were not wrapped in a corn husk or a banana leaf, as they might be in Mexico and other countries in Latin America. They were wrapped in paper and tied with string. They were Chicago corn roll tamales, sold especially at hot dog stands, inexpensive, filling, and tasty enough. The main brand names were, and still are, Supreme and Tom Tom. To this day, these tamales are commonly available at hot dog stands all over the city.

The Chicago corn roll tamale is made on a machine that extrudes the cornmeal tube with a core of lightly seasoned meat (although sometimes those darker centers seem to be just cornmeal, mixed with fat and tinted a brownish red). Unlike traditional tamales that are made in family kitchens or in the back rooms of Mexican restaurants, the Chicago corn roll tamale is an industrial product. You won't find anything like it in Mexico.

The Supreme Company has trademarked the name "The Chicago Tamale," and they carry several varieties including corn roll tamales (meatless, though there is a core that looks like meat), chicken tamales, and beef tamales, which the USDA has determined use enough meat to actually earn their designation as "beef."

THANK YOU, GREAT MIGRATION

According to the Southern Foodways Alliance, the tamale was brought to the United States by Mexican workers who shoved a few tamales in their pockets before going off to work in the fields. In those fields, specifically in the Mississippi Delta, Mexicans would have encountered African Americans with whom, perhaps, they shared their tamales.

Tamales were probably enjoyed in Chicago before the Great Migration from the Delta to Chicago, when African Americans brought the tamales with them. Though it's unknown when, exactly, tamales started being sold on the streets of Chicago, one of the first recorded instances of tamales in Chicago was at the World's Columbian Exposition in 1893. The vendors at the Exposition, though not much is known about them, were likely Mexican.

The African American community in Chicago and elsewhere also had its tamale vendors, as evidenced by some of the sheet music dealing with tamales, now housed in Duke University's Historic American Sheet Music collection. The hot tamale was immortalized in 1936 by Delta bluesman Robert Johnson, he of the Faustian bargain at the crossroads, in the song "They're Red Hot":

> Hot tamales and they're red hot, yes, she got 'em for sale.
> Hot tamales and they're red hot, yes, she got 'em for sale.

I got a girl, say she long and tall,
She sleeps in the kitchen with her feets in the hall.
Hot tamales and they're red hot, yes, she got 'em for sale, I mean
Yes, she got 'em for sale, yeah!

The Chicago corn roll tamale is a variation on the Delta tamale, a moister version of the corn tamale brought up north during the Great Migration. Something akin to the Delta tamale was available under the now-discontinued Derby label, which was owned by Swift, a major name in Chicago meat packing. Derby offered a brace of lightly spiced, red and somewhat heavily sauced tamales in a jar, each wrapped in a plasticized paper, and filled with meat including chopped beef tongue. Using this kind of offal (and, we'd guess, other unlisted "fifth quarter" organs and meats) gave meat packers a way to use less-desirable cuts, and as Gustavus Swift himself bragged, his company used "everything but the squeal" of the animals processed at his facilities.

STILL GOING STRONG

Nick Petros, son of Chris Petros, who bought Tom Tom Tamale & Bakery in 1936, said in a 1998 *Chicago Tribune* story, "The Tom Tom tamale is a little different from a Mexican tamale . . . Ours is straight-out cornmeal. And meat in a Mexican tamale is shredded; ours is ground. Because the meat is ground completely, our spices blend more thoroughly."

During a recent call to Tom Tom Tamale & Bakery I spoke with Tony Argyropolus, an employee since 1970. I asked, jokingly, if they eat many tamales in Greece, and he returned the joke, saying, "Well, the Mexican people have started serving gyros, so we had to start making tamales."

Of course, gyros as we now know the food—pressed meat molded into a frustum and browned on a vertical grill—probably arrived in Chicago long after corn roll tamales.

The spread of the corn roll tamale in Chicago was similarly due less to Mexicans and African Americans and more to Greeks and Armenians. The Petros family bought the Tom Tom Tamale & Bakery in the 1930s and the Paklaian family bought Supreme Frozen Products in 1950.

Both Tom Tom and Supreme tamales are still sold in Chicago and its suburbs. One variant of the Chicago tamale that I remember having as a kid, and that's still available at select locations, is the "bunch" tamale. The bunch-style tamale is not a roll, it's a rectangle. The tamale is divided, in an origami-like paper-folding maneuver, into four tender fingers, luscious, golden, and greasy as hell.

Though tamales have been a staple of Chicago street food culture for years, one could not make a strong argument for their deliciousness. In a blind taste test, one would be stymied to distinguish by taste alone the corn meal outer layer and the "meat" interior, sometimes recognizable only by the magenta tint of the beef-flavored filling, though some corn roll tamales are made with ground beef, usually the beef plate, a rather fatty cut that comes between the brisket and flank of the cow.

For lifelong Chicagoans, our version of the tamale carries powerful nostalgic power—and these humble, inexpensive corn roll snacks are also good for filling up that last bit of belly space that might remain after consuming the far meatier hot dog or Italian beef sandwich.

The Chicago corn roll tamale also has a starring role in the Mother-in-Law (chapter 21).

WHERE TO GET A CHICAGO CORN ROLL TAMALE

Chicago corn roll tamales can be found at many grocery stores, but here are some hot dog and Italian beef stands where you can find them.

Portillo's Hot Dogs
100 W. Ontario St.
312-587-8910

Gene and Jude's
2720 River Road
River Grove, IL
708-452-7634

Jay's Beef
4418 N. Narragansett Ave.
Harwood Heights, IL
708-867-6733

CHICAGO MIX

David Hammond

A BLEND OF CARAMEL- AND CHEESE-COATED POPCORN

Garrett Mix, signature tin. Photo: Garrett Popcorn Shops

For centuries, Iroquois and other indigenous peoples of the Midwest used clay pots filled with hot sand to pop dried corn. Mass consumption of popcorn, however, didn't start in earnest until 1893, when Chicago entrepreneur Charles Cretors presented the first popcorn-popping machine at the World's Columbian Exposition. Cretors's steam-powered machine could roast peanuts, coffee, and popcorn. This innovative mechanism turned out product that was very consistent from batch to batch, and the corn-popping process lured customers with the irresistible scent of freshly popped corn. It practically marketed itself!

At Chicago's Columbian Exposition were also two German immigrants, Frederick and Louis Rueckheim, who added peanuts to their molasses-flavored popcorn to create Cracker Jack, which was soon to become a favorite treat at ball games. This boxed confection, with a "prize inside," was immortalized in the song "Take Me Out to the Ballgame," with the line "Buy me some peanuts and Cracker Jack / I don't care if I never get back."

You could make the case that what's traditionally called Chicago Mix—a blend of caramel- and cheese-coated popcorn—is the most popular international food associated with the city of Chicago. Garrett Popcorn Shops have spread around the world, with locations in Chicago (of course!), Las Vegas, Washington, DC, and many other U.S. cities, as well as several shops in Hong Kong, Tokyo, Malaysia, Singapore, Thailand, and the United Arab Emirates. For years, Garrett sold what millions of people around the world, and everyone in Chicago, knew as Chicago Mix.

Walking down any one of several main drags in Chicago—Michigan Avenue, Jackson, Madison, Randolph—you'll feel yourself slowing your pace as you approach one of the Garrett Popcorn Shops. The atmosphere around these shops is heavy with an alluringly sweet and savory aroma, and the big seller is that blend of caramel- and cheese-coated popcorn, now called, thanks to a court order, not Chicago Mix but rather Garrett Mix.

GARRETT MIX WAS ONCE CALLED CHICAGO MIX

According to the Garrett Popcorn Shops website, "Our secret family recipe of real cheddar cheese and oh-so-sweet, buttery caramel will delight your taste buds. Indulge in sweet and savory flavors made in Chicago since 1949."

As confirmed in recent court rulings, a version of Chicago Mix—a three-way blend of caramel and cheese popcorn as well as "seasoned popcorn" (which tastes like simply salted and buttered popcorn)—had also been offered by Candyland of Saint Paul, Minnesota. Candyland, however, trademarked the name in 1992, and now they are the only company that can legally sell anything called "Chicago Mix."

So, who was the first to come out with Chicago Mix? We'd vote for Garrett Popcorn Shops, but there's no doubt that the first to trademark the name "Chicago Mix" was Candyland, and they get credit for legally jumping on an established good thing.

Whoever first had the genius culinary vision to mix caramel- and cheese-coated popcorn, Candyland has the trademark and the legal grounds to assert, as they do on their website, "Don't be fooled: We own the trademark and have successfully defended it! Our product is authentic."

Candyland's lawsuit compelled not only Garrett Popcorn Shops but all other companies to stop using the name "Chicago Mix" or any variation thereof, including "Chi Style" or "Chicago Style." Still, if you Google the name "Chicago Mix," you'll find that some companies continue to offer what they call "Chicago Mix," though it's only a matter of time before more court orders compel them to find another name as well.

Many of us lifelong Chicagoans still refer to Willis Tower as Sears Tower, and sometimes we slip and call Guaranteed Rate Field by the old name, Comiskey. So, ask any Chicagoan where you can buy Chicago Mix, and they'll know just what you're talking about. And it's almost inevitable that they'll tell you that for Chicago Mix, you need to go to Garrett Popcorn Shops.

BUT, REALLY, WHO ACTUALLY "INVENTED" THE COMBO OF CHEESE-CARAMEL POPCORN?

Friend and fellow food enthusiast Dr. Peter Engler brought to our attention an intriguing article from the *Chicago Tribune*, December 12, 1986. In this article, the late film critic Gene Siskel explains his strategy for mixing popcorn for a sublimely delicious snack:

> "Garrett's is a gourmet popcorn shop . . . My recommendation to you—and it may sound disgusting to you as it did to me when I first saw someone order it; but don't let that put you off—is to order a half-and-half mixture of caramel and cheese . . . You get a sweet-and-sour effect that's fabulous. It's not cheap, but the quality is very high."

As with many of the made-in-Chicago foods, the actual inventor of a preparation may be lost in time, but many times it may be just some anonymous person (like the person Siskel saw order what came to be known as the Chicago Mix) who first started eating food prepared a certain way. Soon, a larger commercial concern—like a shop or restaurant—seizes that good idea as their own and establishes themselves as the first to serve it. One cannot say that this is what happened with the Garrett Mix, or Chicago Mix, but Siskel's account suggests that possibility.

WHERE TO GET CHICAGO MIX/GARRETT MIX

There are several stores offering the confection that combines caramel and cheese popcorn.

Candyland has several locations in Minnesota, including:
435 Wabasha St. North
St Paul, Minnesota
651-292-1191

Garrett Popcorn Shops has multiple locations around the world, including:
500 W. Madison St.
888-476-7267

Wells Street Popcorn
1119 Lake St.
Oak Park, Illinois
708-383-1600

HOW TO PREPARE CHICAGO MIX/GARRETT MIX AT HOME

Ingredients

- 30 cups plain popped corn
- 2 cups brown sugar
- ½ cup light corn syrup
- 1½ teaspoon salt
- 1 cup unsalted butter
- ½ teaspoon baking soda
- 2 teaspoons vanilla extract
- 6 tablespoons butter
- ½ cup cheddar cheese powder
- ¼ teaspoon mustard powder
- ½ teaspoon salt

Preparation

Caramel Popcorn

1. Divide the popped corn into two large baking pans.
2. Preheat the oven to 200 degrees Fahrenheit.
3. Combine the brown sugar, corn syrup, salt, and ½ cup butter in a saucepan and bring to a boil over medium heat, stirring enough to blend but not burn.
4. Boil the mixture for 3–4 minutes, stirring constantly.
5. Remove from the heat and stir in the baking soda and vanilla extract.
6. Pour it over the popcorn and stir to coat.
7. Bake for 45 minutes, stirring the popcorn every 15 minutes.
8. When the popcorn comes out of the oven, try to separate the pieces as much as you can before it cools completely.

Cheddar Popcorn

1. Put the remaining popcorn in a paper bag; pour over the corn the remaining ½ cup butter and shake.
2. Combine the cheddar cheese powder, mustard powder, and salt in a small bowl.
3. Sprinkle over the popcorn and shake the bag.

Mix the caramel and cheddar popcorn and serve.

Recipe modified from Sabrina Snyder's "Chicago Mix Cheddar and Caramel Popcorn!" Dinner Then Dessert, May 2, 2019, https://dinnerthendessert.com/chicago-mix-cheddar-caramel-popcorn/.

8

CHICAGO-STYLE EGG ROLL

David Hammond

EGG ROLLS, CHICAGO STYLE, STUFFED WITH JERK CHICKEN AND OTHER UNLIKELY INGREDIENTS

3 King's Jerk. Photo: David Hammond

Sitting in front of 3 Kings Jerk on Chicago's West Side, I wasn't entirely sure if the place was open. It was one p.m. on a Tuesday, so the small storefront restaurant should have been open, but I couldn't quite see if the lights were on. From my car, I tried to peer around the cage-like red bars that covered the front windows, attempting to detect some movement inside. Finally, I saw the flash of a person by the counter, so I got out and walked in. Behind the counter, two nice ladies were making egg rolls to order, which is the way it should be: an egg roll that sits around cooling off will be way less delicious than one right out of the fryer. The ladies here take their egg rolls seriously.

The broad and impressive menu at 3 Kings Jerk offers chicken jerked and fried, as well as jerk dinners of chicken and fish, oxtails, and lamb chops. There are also many tacos and "fresh egg rolls." With all these ingredients around, it's almost inevitable that someone, someday, was going to put a few of them together just to see what would happen.

Like the taco, the egg roll seems to be one of those infinitely variable carbohydrate platforms that can become the vehicle for any meat and vegetable combination the cook decides to use. And who are these egg roll cooks? They're usually employees of one of Chicago's many storefront Chinese restaurants.

The egg rolls prepared at most of Chicago's Chinese restaurants—whether storefront or sit-down—contain one ingredient that might surprise out-of-towners, but which Chicagoans have come to expect: peanut butter.

A few years ago, Louisa Chu wrote in the *Chicago Tribune* that "The Chicago-style egg roll may look like any version of the iconic Chinese American tubular appetizer: deep fried until golden brown, bubbly, and crunchy on the outside, with cabbage plus sometimes pork, shrimp, and other ingredients on the inside. The defining ingredient of the Chicago-style egg roll, however, is a hint of peanut butter in the filling . . . the peanut butter–flavored egg rolls are not only in Chicago, though they are primarily found here."

The big question, of course, is why? Why add peanut butter to the eggrolls? There are several theories for this unorthodox ingredient: the peanut butter may help bind the ingredients together (doesn't really seem necessary as the fried tube contains the ingredients quite well) or it may help to hold the egg roll wrapper in place (a brush with the namesake egg would achieve the same objective). Or maybe peanut butter is added for the flavor. Sometimes, you can taste the peanut butter and it's kind of . . . nice. This should not be surprising: peanuts are added to many Southeast Asian dishes (think pad Thai), and the goober is quite complementary to many ingredients, Asian and otherwise.

Chicago chefs, particularly Black chefs, however, have been pushing beyond peanut butter and way beyond the boundaries of the traditional Chinese egg roll. As Nick Kindelsperger wrote in the *Tribune*: "if you wander around predominantly Black neighborhoods on the West and South sides, you'll notice a completely different kind of egg roll—one that uses the same wrapper, but then leaves nearly everything else behind. The most common filling for these egg rolls is jerk chicken, and since it began to pop up in the city five years ago, it has become nearly ubiquitous on menus of Black-owned restaurants and dozens of non-Chinese establishments across the city."

At 3 Kings Jerk, they sell a lot of jerk chicken, and such spicy meat worked quite well in an eggroll. With tiny flecks of cabbage and carrot, a jerk chicken egg roll is piquant and filling (particularly if you go for the jumbo version, which is about two-and-one-half times larger than a regular egg roll).

The whole thing gets a little weirder and more interesting when you consider the list of ingredients that places like 3 Kings Jerk put into egg rolls: garlic parmesan chicken, Buffalo chicken, Philly cheese steak, shrimp and broccoli, gyros, and shrimp, and . . . Italian beef.

For dessert, taffy grapes (see chapter 29), another Chicago original snack that tastes particularly good after spicy food, is on the menu at some of the restaurants serving Chicago-style egg rolls.

Get yourself an Italian beef egg roll and a cup of taffy grapes and there you have it, a trifecta of Chicago foods in one meal: the Italian beef, the nontraditional Chicago-style egg roll, and a tasty after-dinner snack.

WHERE TO GET A CHICAGO-STYLE EGG ROLL

3 Kings Jerk
5451 W. Madison St.
773-688-5525

Kathryn's Soul
131 N. Clinton St.
773-231-0782

The Soul Shack
1368 E. 53rd St.
773-891-0126

9

CHICAGO HOT DOG

Monica Eng

A WIENER (BOILED, SIMMERED, OR STEAMED) IN A STEAMED POPPY SEED BUN, TOPPED WITH YELLOW MUSTARD, CHOPPED ONIONS, NEON-GREEN RELISH, TOMATOES, DILL PICKLES, SPORT PEPPERS, AND CELERY SALT

Chicago-style hot dog. Photo: Monica Eng

It starts with a snappy all-beef wiener nestled in a steamed poppy seed bun. Then comes a squirt of yellow mustard, chopped onions, neon-green relish, slices of tomato, a dill pickle spear, sport peppers (usually two), and a final whoosh of celery salt.

When all these elements harmonize on one bun, they unleash a symphony of flavors that sing with Chicago history.

But how did this peculiar bunch of ingredients come to define the Chicago hot dog?

I went in search of the answer years ago for the Curious City show at WBEZ and found that you can indeed teach an old Chicago food writer new tricks.

My main source was Bruce Kraig, a retired food historian and author of the books *Man Bites Dog* and *Hot Dog: A Global History*. Kraig explained that the hot dog was not really "invented" by a single person. Instead, it was shaped by a parade of cultural influences that tell the story of early twentieth-century immigration to Chicago—especially to the Maxwell Street Market area, around Halsted Street and Roosevelt Road.

I subsequently talked to a few other Chicago hot dog experts, who confirmed Kraig's theories, but also added some extra flavor of their own to the hot dog story.

DID ABE DREXLER REALLY INVENT THE CHICAGO DOG?

This is a popular theory and one that posits that Abe Drexler, who founded the Fluky's hot dog stand on Maxwell Street in 1929, came up with the canonical Chicago hot dog, but Kraig says, "there isn't really any evidence for that."

Instead, the food scholar notes that the super-specific Chicago style ingredients took time to settle into their final combo—and evolved into their current canonical formation between 1920 and 1950 (though the neon-green color of the relish may have been a later development).

"By the 1930s, hot dog stands that were fixed and permanent (as opposed to rolling pushcarts) served something like this style—not always with everything," Kraig said. "But then this final style evolved after World War II and was part of Chicago's move to big [industrial] food, for which the city is famous."

WIENER

Kraig explains that the hot dog itself "descends from a broad variety of sausages brought by German immigrants who came to the States in great numbers beginning in the 1850s, and many settled in Chicago over the next fifty years."

Those early sausages, however, were mostly mixtures of pork and beef.

"But another immigrant group beginning in the 1890s were Jews from Eastern Europe (especially Hungary and Austria) who did not eat pork, and they took up the sausage business in companies like Vienna, making all-beef sausages. So, in Chicago—the beef capital of America at the time—that became the Chicago style."

Vienna Beef CEO Jim Bodman says the final recipe for the classic Vienna frank was mostly settled in the early twentieth century.

"We have formulas that go back to the early 1900s," he said. "But back then they sort of did things through touch . . . They would stick their finger into [the meat mixture] and say, for example, 'we need more bull meat, give me another shovel of bull meat.'"

You read that right. Bodman said they add chewy bull meat—from uncastrated steers—to give Chicago-style franks their classic "snap and bounce."

"If you had a steak made of bull meat you could barely chew it . . . because it is laden with myosin protein," he said. "So, we take this bull meat, and we mix it up with what we call fifty-fifty trimmings that are half meat [from cows and steers], half fat."

In the end, he says, the wiener ends up consisting of 20 percent fat and 80 percent meat. But "when you bite into a really good hot dog and it kind of bites you back," he says, "well that's the bull meat."

BUN

According to Kraig, Chicago's steamed poppy seed bun is a product of Teutonic influence.

"Germans always ate sausages on bread," he said. "And the earliest bun evidence we have is from New York—from a special bun maker on Coney Island as early as the 1870s. The poppy seeds are from Jewish East Europeans, and they didn't become popular [on the Chicago dog bun] until after World War II."

MUSTARD

Food historian Kraig says this yellow addition is also a product of German immigrants.

"Mustard always went with sausages," he told me as we talked for a 2017 WBEZ story. "Germans have been masters of mustard from the beginning and (this blander) yellow one is derived from the stronger ones in Germany that became mass manufactured by the end of the nineteenth century for the American audience. And it was cheap."

RELISH

No one I talked to is quite sure why or when Chicago's relish took on such a vibrantly green hue, but its origins go back to yet another favorite way to preserve cucumbers and accent a meal.

"The relish was originally called piccalilli and it's an old English recipe," Kraig said. "The [German] analog here would be sauerkraut, but this is sweeter because it has sugar in it. So, it's an old timey American country recipe. The earliest evidence I've seen for relish piccalilli on a hot dog comes from a 1928 exhibition game between the Sox and Cubs."

CHOPPED RAW ONIONS

Kraig said the addition of onions on the hot dog could have come from any one of the European groups who populated the Maxwell Street area in the early twentieth century.

"Onions are pan-European," he noted. "All Eastern European and South Europeans like Greeks and Italians used them," so they may all have been responsible for the topping.

TOMATOES

Bob Schwartz, a vice president at Vienna Beef and the author of *Never Put Ketchup on a Hot Dog*, said tomato slices were the last ingredients to join the Chicago hot dog canon.

"The original Depression Dog was mustard, onions, relish, cucumbers and peppers," he said. "The tomato came later."

And he said he doesn't mind it because, at least, "it wasn't sweet like ketchup."

But who decided to add those tomatoes?

"The slices of tomatoes come from the combination of Jews, Greeks, and Italians all living together near Maxwell Street, and all vying for control of the fruit vegetable market," Kraig said. "And so, somebody thought they should put tomatoes on the dogs as an added value. And, of course, they also look good against the bright green relish."

PICKLE SPEAR

Schwartz said the pickle spear was another latish addition that took the place of the fresh cucumber on the original dog. But the influences that put it there were clear.

"The dill pickle is absolutely Central and East European, and universally American," Kraig told me in 2017 for my hot dog story. "Every old cookbook that had piccalilli in it also had pickles in it. American farmers, and Americans, generally, loved eating pickles."

SPORT PEPPERS

There are differing theories on how these spicy little devils got on the Chicago-style dog.

Schwartz believes they came up to Chicago in the late 1930s with African American migrants.

"The sport peppers came with the Great Migration," he said, "with people moving from the South to the North and bringing these peppers that are from Louisiana."

But Kraig thinks they may have come from an earlier group of visitors.

"They probably came up when the railroad was built to Mexico in the 1870s," he said. "Also, during the Colombian Exposition there were tamale sellers, and they were selling Mexican tamales with chiles. So, there was a taste in Chicago for these hot peppers, and they went right on to hot dogs."

CELERY SALT

Kraig believes the final dusting of celery salt came to us courtesy of a certain health craze sweeping the nation in the early twentieth century.

"Celery was once a major American vegetable promoted by every health food guru as 'good for you,' particularly since they were very interested in chewing," he said.

And believe it or not, Chicago's North Side was a huge U.S. celery hub due to our train lines and sandy soil. But instead of putting a celery stalk on a dog, Kraig said hot dog stands opted to "at least have this processed celery product."

NO KETCHUP?

You know how Schwartz (author of *Never Put Ketchup on a Hot Dog*) feels about the red condiment, but I asked Kraig if he'd ever entertain the thought of putting this sweet sauce on a Chicago dog.

The answer was an unequivocal "No."

"There is a culinary reason, in my opinion, for this," he said. "If you consider what's on a Chicago-style hot dog, it is hot, sour, salty, sweet altogether with crunchy vegetables in a soft bun. So, it's a symphony of textures and flavors unmatched anywhere. And if you put ketchup on it, it will kill everything."

MORE ABOUT THE DEPRESSION DOG

One unsung partner to the classic Chicago hot dog is the Depression Dog, so named because it reflects the privations of the Great Depression in the United States and may have achieved popularity during that period. It's the hot dog preparation Chicagoans used to buy at pushcarts in Chicago public parks before those relics of a past era vanished.

The Depression Dog, as still served at places like the legendary Gene & Jude's, is simply a thin sausage, nestled in a seedless bun, covered with mustard, chopped onion, relish, and optional sport peppers, but without pickles, tomatoes, or celery salt.

A COUPLE MORE CHICAGO DOG BITES

Other local variations on the hot dog include the Francheezie, an all-beef jumbo wiener stuffed with melted American cheese and wrapped in bacon—sometimes deep fried. Although we don't know its exact origin, this very nonkosher creation was popular at local delis in the mid-twentieth century. Today you can find it at the Bagel Restaurant and Deli on Broadway, the Pittsfield Cafe, and the Riverview Diner in Montgomery, Illinois.

Many Chicagoans also love the "char dog," which uses the same all-beef frank but crosscuts the ends before cooking on a real charcoal grill. Kraig suggests that they came into fashion at some hot dog stands with the mid-century rise of backyard grilling in America. You can find them at North Side spots including Wolfy's, the Wiener's Circle, and Charcoal Delights. A variation called the "char cheddar dog" includes a smear of cheese spread.

WHERE TO GET DEPRESSION DOGS AND CHICAGO-STYLE HOT DOGS

Gene and Jude's
(Depression Dogs)
2720 N River Rd.
River Grove, IL
708-452-7634

Jimmy's Red Hots
(Depression Dogs)
4000 W. Grand Ave.
773-384-9513

Byron's Hot Dogs
(Classic Chicago Hot Dogs)
1701 W Lawrence Ave.
773-271-0900

Red Hot Ranch
(Classic Chicago Hot Dogs)
2449 W. Armitage Ave.
773-772-6020

DEEP DISH PIZZA

David Hammond

CHEESE AND "TOPPINGS" WITH TOMATO SAUCE ON THE TOP, BAKED INTO A FIRM, HIGH-SIDED PIE

Lou Malnati's deep dish pizza. Photo: Steve Dolinsky

We in the land of the Big Mac have supersized our deli sandwiches, our soft drinks, our pizzas. The perfect example of the all-American "more is better" approach is the deep dish pizza, a combination of two of our favorite things—cheese and sausage—in a baked dough bowl that's on the other end of the crust spectrum from the paper-thin Margherita made in Naples, the generally recognized birthplace of pizza, or the thin-crust tavern-style pizza (chapter 30) that's probably Chicago's most popular version of the pie.

Deep dish pizza is cooked in a pan that gives each pie a side crust that's an inch or so high. To prepare the pie, the dough is pressed into the pan and up along the sides. Ingredients are then added in this order: cheese; fillings (such as sausage, green peppers, or mushrooms); finally, tomato sauce is ladled on top. After baking, the pie is cut into large slices (so that all the ingredients stay in place). In each slice, you can see the distinct strata of cheese and "toppings" (in the center) with tomato sauce on the top, all baked into a firm, high-sided pie.

A friend from France visited recently. It was her first time in Chicagoland, and she had one thing on her mind: deep dish pizza. She, like so many first-time visitors to the city, was eager to try the food that most non-Chicagoans feel they simply must have when they finally reach the Windy City. For what it's worth, she liked it.

During a WGN radio broadcast in 2019, I sat on a panel with Steve Dolinsky, broadcast food journalist and author of *Pizza City, USA* and *The Ultimate Chicago Pizza Guide*. Dolinsky mentioned that if you go down the line at Uno's Pizzeria and Grill or Pizzeria Due, two of Chicago's classic deep dish pizza places, you'll find "that most of the people waiting for deep dish pizza are from out of town." To many lifelong Chicagoans, deep dish pizza is now mostly a dish for tourists, though even those of us who were born here indulge in a slice (slab is more like it) of deep dish pizza maybe once or twice a year.

When I was a teenager, we'd sometimes go to Uno's or Due's for a deep dish or two. In those days, my friends and I could each put away a few thousand calories at a single meal, no problem. Now, such a food orgy has little appeal, though I must say, when out-of-town visitors blow in looking for this classic Chicago specialty, we're always happy to oblige.

As with Italian beef (chapter 15) and so many other Chicago original foods, there's much contention around the questions of "who invented deep dish pizza?"

IT'S NOT EASY TO FIGURE OUT WHO INVENTED DEEP DISH PIZZA

Go to the website for Uno's and you'll find this claim: "We're the guys who invented deep dish. . . It all began when Chicago businessman Ike Sewell imagined a pizza unlike any other. Fresh dough with a tall edge, topped with homemade sauce and more cheese than you could believe. People have been lining up ever since."

Then browse Lou Malnati's website, and you'll see: "Lou Malnati's Pizzerias have stayed true to the original Chicago-style deep dish pizza recipe that Grandpa

Malnati helped create in 1943 at Chicago's first deep dish pizzeria." The "first deep dish pizzeria" mentioned here is Uno's.

The now conventional wisdom about its origins, namely that Sewell invented it, should be put straight. Sewell's partner, Italian-born Ric Riccardo (born Navoretti), who owned Riccardo's bar and restaurant on Rush Street, deserves some of the credit. Pulitzer Prize–winning true-blue Chicago author and historian Studs Terkel, as quoted by Dolinsky in *Pizza City, USA*, is reported to have said about the deep dish pie, "Ric invented the f***ing pizza for God's sake."

Unfortunately, Riccardo died in 1951 and did not have a chance to tell his side of the story, and the story has only become more Sewell-centric over the years.

Even as recently as 1986, when Sewell was interviewed by *Chicago Tribune* reporter Paul Galloway, he recalled that when Riccardo came back from a trip to Italy, he had insisted they open a pizzeria and even cooked a test pizza for Sewell.

Sewell reportedly said, "It's great, but it won't sell. It's more like an appetizer. We need something more to feed people than this. But Riccardo was adamant [about making it a pizzeria]. And so, we started experimenting."

In the end, so the story goes, they dreamed up something of their own. "Before this, pizzas had been thrown in the oven like a little piece of dough on a flat pan. We have these deep dish pans made up for us, and we open (the present) Pizzeria Uno with pizza cooked this way and as a full meal, which had never been done before. We added Italian salad, tortoni ice cream as dessert, and Italian coffee."

This admission is a far cry from the full credit given to Sewell in many places, including the Pizzeria Uno website. But, according to City of Chicago cultural historian Tim Samuelson, this 1986 account is still too generous to Sewell.

When my coauthor Monica Eng wrote to Samuelson to ask if he'd heard that Riccardo was indeed the brain behind the pie, he wrote this back.

"Yes. . . . Ric Riccardo was the person behind opening what was originally called 'The Pizzeria' at Ohio and Wabash—and its evolution into Pizzeria Riccardo and Pizzeria Uno in the same location. Although there are many colorful stories about Ike Sewell collaborating with Riccardo at the outset, he didn't come into the picture until slightly after 'The Pizzeria' was opened. And there is ample documentation of Riccardo figuring out an unconventional type of pizza as a signature dish for his new bar/restaurant opened in 1943, as well as written descriptions of him demonstrating how to make one of these behemoths."

Ike Sewell was a colorful Texas-style storyteller, and his own descriptions of his role with Riccardo and the pizza became more elaborate over the years. I don't regard it as deception—he was involved so early in the pizzeria's operation that he got some of the facts conflated over time.

But there may be yet another side to this story.

Writing in *Eater*, Dan Zemans came to an unorthodox yet compelling interpretation of the origins of deep dish pizza. According to Zemans, the problem with the story that Sewell or Ricardo invented the deep dish pizza "is that there is zero evidence to support the notion that two guys with no known cooking acumen came up with the recipe for deep dish pizza. In fact, there's no record of anyone ever claiming to have seen either one of them even making a pizza. So, if not them, then who? Well, there are two better possibilities: Adolpho 'Rudy' Malnati Sr. and Alice May Redmond. Not only did both work at Uno's but each of them unquestionably knew how to make pizza.

"Malnati, and later his sons and grandsons, went on to own and operate over sixty locations (as of early 2022) of Lou Malnati's Pizzeria, the most extensive of all the deep dish empires. Redmond went on to cook deep dish pizza at Gino's East, though her name, most unfairly, has faded from the annals of Chicago food history."

Based on what we know today, it seems that Malnati and Redmond played pivotal roles in what came to be called the Chicago deep dish pizza. As with Chicago-invented dishes like chicken Vesuvio and shrimp DeJonghe, it's also possible that Chicago deep dish pizza was inspired by homestyle dishes that were not initially made in a restaurant kitchen. Italian bakeries had long sold thick squares of "pizza bread," topped with tomato sauce and cheese. Pizza bread came before Chicago deep dish pizza, but whether it inspired Redmond or Malnati, we will likely never know.

STUFFED PIZZA, SON OF DEEP DISH

Stuffed pizza bears a resemblance to deep dish, with two main differences. Stuffed features a thicker layer of cheese, sometimes full of spinach, broccoli, or pesto, and it has a very, very thin top crust positioned on top of the "toppings" and underneath the upper layer of tomato sauce. This almost indiscernible top crust tends to get lost in the tomato sauce, and you usually must make an effort to find it. On a recent stuffed pizza we had, we could not find any top crust, though we were assured that it was there, somewhere.

In 1974, Giordano's Pizza and Nancy's Pizza opened; both offered the "first" stuffed pizza in Chicago and probably the world.

WHERE TO GET A DEEP DISH PIZZA

Uno's Pizzeria & Grill, Pizzeria Due (many national locations, including this one)
619 N. Wabash St.
312-943-2400

Lou Malnati's Pizzeria (many national locations, including this one)
6649 N. Lincoln Ave.
Lincolnwood, IL
847-673-0800

Gino's East
2801 N. Lincoln Ave.
773-327-3737

WHERE TO GET STUFFED PIZZA

Giordano's Pizza (many national locations, including this one)
730 N. Rush St.
312-951-0747

Nancy's Pizzeria
1000 W. Washington Blvd.
312-733-9920

HOW TO MAKE DEEP DISH PIZZA AT HOME

Serves 6–8

Choose a 10-inch heavy round cake pan with 2-inch high sides to make this pizza. A 10-inch springform pan works well, too; when you remove the side of the pan, it's easy to cut and serve the pizza. Generously grease the pan with vegetable oil. Sprinkle the bottom of the pan with cornmeal; set aside.

CRUST

Ingredients

1 cup warm water (120–130 degrees Fahrenheit)
1 package active dry years
3 cups flour
⅓ cup vegetable oil
½ teaspoon salt

Procedure

1. In a large bowl, combine warm water and yeast; stir to dissolve. Let stand 5 minutes, and then stir in 1½ cups flour, vegetable oil, and salt.
2. Beat with an electric mixer on low speed for 30 seconds, scraping the sides of the bowl constantly; then beat on high speed for 2 minutes.
3. Use a wooden spoon to stir in the remaining 1½ cups flour.
4. Turn the dough out onto a lightly floured surface and knead in extra flour to make a moderately stiff dough that is smooth and elastic (may take up to 8 minutes to get this right).
5. Shape dough into a ball and place in a lightly greased bowl, turning once to thoroughly grease the surface of the dough.
6. Cover and let it rise in a warm place until double in size (may take an hour). Punch down dough; cover and allow to rest for 5 minutes.
7. Place dough in the prepared pan. Using oiled hands, press and spread the dough evenly over the bottom and 1½ inches up the sides of pan. Cover and let rise in a warm place until double in size (may take up to 35 minutes).

FILLING

Ingredients

12 ounces bulk Italian sausage
1 cup onion, chopped
8 ounces pizza sauce

4 ounces canned mushrooms, drained
3½ ounces sliced pepperoni
2 teaspoons dried basil
1 teaspoons dried oregano

Procedure

1. Cook sausage and brown onion in pan, then drain
2. Stir in pizza sauce, mushrooms, pepperoni, basil, and oregano

ASSEMBLE AND BAKE

Ingredients

12 ounces mozzarella, sliced
¼ cup Parmesan, grated

Procedure

1. Preheat oven to 375 degrees Fahrenheit.
2. Arrange mozzarella slices over the inside surface of the dough.
3. Spoon the filling over the mozzarella cheese and sprinkle with grated Parmesan cheese.
4. Bake for 45 to 55 minutes or until the edge of the crust is crispy golden and the filling is heated through. To avoid a burnt crust, cover the edge of the crust with foil for the last 10 minutes of baking.
5. Cool pizza on a wire rack for 10 minutes. If using a springform pan, remove the sides of the pan.
6. Cut pizza into pie-shaped wedges.

Recipe modified from Better Homes & Gardens, "How to Make a Deep Dish Pizza," June 9, 2015, https://www.bhg.com/recipes/pizza/how-to-make-deep-dish-pizza/.

FLAMING SAGANAKI

David Hammond

FLAMING GREEK CHEESE IN A PAN, SERVED WITH AN "OPA!"

Saganaki at Avli Trattoria. Photo: Kailley Lindman

Standing in line outside Dianna's Opaa! at 212 South Halsted in Greektown in the mid-1970s, you'd have seen owner and überhost Petros Kogeones working the line, shaking the men's hands, kissing all the ladies, offering everyone a complimentary shot of ouzo. He was a good-looking man, long black hair, shirt unbuttoned just a little further down than seemed necessary, a gold chain around his neck, an Adonis for the disco era.

Once inside Kogeones's restaurant, you'd see him dancing, sometimes balancing a water glass on his head, randomly shouting "Opa!" Kogeones was a powerful promoter, and according to him, he was also the inventor of flaming saganaki, the flambéed fromage now found in Greek restaurants the world over. He was most definitely a Chicago character.

Harry Mark Petrakis is the Greek American author who wrote the novel *A Dream of Kings*, which was later made into a movie starring Anthony Quinn and is set in part in Chicago's Greektown. Petrakis has a revealing anecdote (or two) about Kogeones, as he explained in an email exchange. "I used to frequent the Kogeoneses' restaurant, where they would always fuss over me. My brother-in-law, George Perparos, ate there once, and when he went to the register to pay his check, he mentioned to Petros, 'You know, Harry Petrakis is my brother-in-law.' Petros tore up his check.

"About a year later George was again in the restaurant, and when he went to pay his check, he told Petros, 'You remember, I ate here last year. I'm Harry Petrakis's brother-in-law.' Apparently Petros had been assaulted by my friends and relatives using my name. He smiled at George and with a dramatic flourish, declared, 'For you . . . No tax!'

"'There was also an episode at the restaurant when we arrived and Petros hugged us all and told us to sit and eat. I thanked him but told him we had just eaten. Petros pulled a gun from beneath his apron and put it to his head, exclaiming. 'If you don't sit down and eat, I'll shoot myself!'"

The Petrakis family relented and ordered some pastry.

But back to the saganaki: According to a 1991 article in the *Chicago Tribune*, "The history of Dianna's goes back to the early 1960s when Petros and his brother Peter put tables in the front of Peter's grocery, in old Greektown, at Halsted and Harrison. Petros was a student at the time, and he brought friends from Navy Pier College [the original location of the University of Illinois in Chicago], and the rest of the outside world followed. The Kogeones brothers doused cheese pie appetizers with brandy, lit it and cried 'Opa!' which Petros described as the Greek exclamation of approval." This was flaming saganaki, Chicago style, and the "doused cheese pie" referred to was not a pie in the traditional American sense but rather a slab of warm cheese, usually chewy, and a little crusty from the quick flaming in the pan.

The word "saganaki" comes from the Greek word for a small pan with two handles: sagani. Foods cooked in this small pan become saganaki (-aki is a diminutive suffix in Greek, like the "y" in Davey or Danny). There are now many types of saganaki, including scallop saganaki and shrimp saganaki. In Chicago, saganaki usually means flaming cheese, though some Chicagoland restaurants serve the un-flamed version.

Pan-seared saganaki is traditional in Greece; the flaming saganaki is a beautiful example of a traditional food that has been modified by Chicagoans to pique the interest of diners. The flaming of the cheese and the accompanying "Opa!" seems designed more to market the menu item than to improve its flavor, though the brandy does offer another dimension of flavor to the cheese, and it's a fun and celebratory dish to have before dinner.

In Greece, you would find lots of different types of cheese—including kasseri, feta, and halloumi—warmed up in a pan, much as the French might warm dishes of raclette cheese. Dry cheeses like kasseri are preferred because they don't melt all over the place. These drier cheeses maintain their shape despite the hot pan and flaming finale before serving.

The Chicago innovation was to set the whole thing on fire before serving it to the customer. Igniting the cheese involves splashing it with brandy. Kogeones claimed this as his own creative twist on a classic, but there is the inevitable dispute on that point.

NOT SO FAST, PETROS . . .

Petros Kogeones seems to have been the most vocal proponent of the idea that he was the inventor of the flaming Greek cheese. The signature "Opa!" is even in the name of his Opaa! restaurant (though in Petros' typical over-the-top style, he added an extra "a" at the end). But like so many Chicago original foods—Italian beef (chapter 15), Mother-in-Law (chapter 21), deep dish pizza (chapter 10), and others—origin stories are frequently contested; success has many parents.

The other vocal claimant to the title "Originator of Flaming Saganaki" is the Parthenon at 314 South Halsted. Indeed, most writers on the topic of saganaki seem to side with the Parthenon's version of saganaki's origin story. In *Lost Restaurants of Chicago*, Greg Borzo recognizes that "The bygone Parthenon . . . is widely credited with inventing in 1968 the Flaming Saganaki and 'Opa' custom."

Parthenon owner Chris Liakouras was quoted in the *Chicago Tribune* as saying, "I invented saganaki at this table in 1968. I was sitting here with three lady friends. We were talking about different things we could do. When a cheese dish was mentioned, one of the ladies said, 'Why don't you try flaming it?'"

After over forty-eight years in business, The Parthenon closed in 2016 for reasons that were never fully disclosed. Flaming saganaki, of course, lives on at many Chicago restaurants.

OPA! DEFINED

I had heard that the Greek expression "Opa!" might be translated as "Oops!" That interpretation certainly seemed possible, and I had intended to check this out with Harry Mark Petrakis, but alas, he passed away in early 2021. I was able to connect with his niece, Dena Manta, a fluent speaker of Greek, and she told me that "Opa means 'Up, get up!' Or it can be a shout of joy when something fun/great is about to happen; when an old person struggles to get up, they say 'Opa!' As regards the flaming cheese (my VERY favorite!), Opa means 'Let the flame rise up!'"

WHERE TO EAT FLAMING SAGANAKI

Athena Restaurant
212 S. Halsted
312-655-0000

Avli Restaurant
566 Chestnut St.
Winnetka, IL
847-446-9300

Greek Islands
200 S. Halsted
312-782-9855

HOW TO PREPARE FLAMING SAGANAKI AT HOME

Serves 1

Ingredients

4-ounce slice of firm, dry Greek cheese (kasseri seems frequently to be the choice)
¼ cup water
¼ cup white flour
1 tablespoon olive oil
2 tablespoons brandy (ouzo is traditional)
¼ lemon

Procedure

1. Brush the cheese slice with water and dredge in flour.
2. Add olive oil to a small, clean pan and preheat.
3. As soon as the olive oil starts smoking, place the cheese onto the pan to quickly brown.
4. Flip cheese when the first side is brown; when second side is brown, add brandy and quickly light.
5. Shout "Opa!" and squirt lemon over the top to help extinguish the flames.
6. Serve with lemon slices and crusty bread.

12

GIARDINIERA

David Hammond

HOT CHILI PEPPERS, CELERY, SWEET PEPPER, AND OTHER VEGETABLES IN OIL

Giardiniera on an Italian beef. Photo: David Hammond

Johnnie's Beef in Elmwood Park always comes in near the top of people's lists of "must visit" Italian beef (chapter 15) joints. When I stop by at Johnnie's, and it's my turn at the register, I always ask for my sandwich "sweet and hot."

At Johnnie's and other Italian beef places, if you say you want your sandwich "sweet," your beef will be adorned with some lightly cooked sweet peppers (almost always green, rather than red or yellow). If you say you want your sandwich "hot," you're going to receive it ladled with giardiniera, a blend of hot chili peppers, celery, sweet pepper, and sometimes other vegetables—maybe carrots and cauliflower—marinated in oil and sometimes vinegar. I usually get both sweet and hot.

In the Italian language, a female gardener is a "giardiniera," and this vegetable-forward condiment is appropriately named after those who garden. Much like the greenery on a dragged-through-the-garden Chicago hot dog (chapter 9), giardiniera's vegetable mix adds a fresh and bright crunch, as well as chili heat (in many versions, though some stands offer mild giardiniera), to a protein-centric, unabashedly and deliciously fatty sandwich.

Like the Italian beef, you'll not likely find this Chicago style of giardiniera in Italy. You will, however, find a condiment that's close: the traditional Italian version of giardiniera contains the cut-up vegetables pickled in vinegar, usually without oil or hot chili peppers.

According to Dalanti, a company that specializes in Italian condiments, "Common vegetables in the Italian version, also called *sotto aceti*, include onions, celery, zucchini, carrots and cauliflower, pickled vegetables in red or white wine vinegar. It is typically eaten as an antipasto, or with salads."

In Chicago, however, giardiniera is a condiment, and Chicago-style giardiniera is commonly made with chopped serrano peppers (sometimes called "sport" peppers in Chicago); with other assorted vegetables, such as bell peppers, olives, celery, pimentos, carrots, and cauliflower, and sometimes crushed red pepper flakes, all marinated in vegetable, soybean, or occasionally olive oil.

Though folklore characterizes Italian tastes as favoring a "spicy meatball," Italians are somewhat heat averse. You may find red pepper flakes on some Italian tables, but you will rarely find the tongue-numbing hot sauce favored by some of us Americans. (Incidentally, our love of chili heat may be attributable to Mexican immigrants to this country; these transplanted chiliheads make a good portion of their traditionally delicious and immensely popular food with hot chili peppers. We in the United States have come to seek out the burn.)

Oil and the chili heat are key to what makes Chicago-style giardiniera different from traditional Italian giardiniera, and across Chicagoland you will find slight variations between the giardiniera sold at Italian beef places and on grocery store shelves. The giardiniera at Johnnie's Beef, for instance, is hotter than the giardiniera that's currently served at Al's #1 Italian Beef, which stopped using serranos in the 1970s, when they started using pepper flakes in a version that contained just celery and spices. The hottest giardiniera we've had is Serrelli's brand, made at Serrelli's Finer Foods, right down the street from Johnnie's. Serrelli's version of giardiniera is blisteringly hot, perhaps too hot for some, so here's a pro tip: at Italian beef stands, if you're not a fan of intense heat, ask the person making up your

Italian beef to sprinkle the meat with the oil—and just the oil—from the giardiniera. This oily essence of giardiniera provides pleasing heat without firebombing your tongue.

Chicago-style giardiniera has limited distribution, and although a version of giardiniera is offered under the name "hot peppers" at Potbelly Sandwich Shops, giardiniera is so much more than just the peppers.

Giardiniera is an excellent, versatile condiment. The bright acidity of the pickled vegetables complements meat, and it can be used on many dishes. We've had it on pizza, in eggs, on a submarine sandwich, and with steak. Giardiniera is also offered on the Jim Shoe (chapter 17), and some Chicagoans even save the oil for cooking and have incorporated it into recipes for pork chops and pot roast. It's a very flexible ingredient that makes the flavor of many dishes come alive.

Giardiniera also adds a lot of color to a sandwich. The drab uniformity of the brown meat slices on an Italian beef sandwich is rendered more colorful and delicious-looking with the addition of glistening vegetables in Chicago-style giardiniera.

WHERE DID GIARDINIERA COME FROM?

The Dalanti site explains, "Chicago-style Giardiniera was invented . . . in 1925 by famous 'Beef and Sausage Man' Pasquale Scala. It's also commonly served on Italian sausage sandwiches, meatball sandwiches, Italian subs and pizza." For years, the Scala Packing Company supplied many of Chicago's Italian beef stands.

However, there are competing origin stories.

Jeff Johnson, the grandson of Vincenzo Formusa, who founded the Marconi company in 1898, claims grandfather Formusa made the first giardiniera. In 2020, the Marconi company sold 3.2 million pounds of the stuff.

Randy Formella, grandson of Enrico Formella, who founded E. Formella and Sons, claims *his* grandfather brought the recipe from Sicily and started making giardiniera in Chicago between 1906 and 1909. In 2020, Formella sold 8.1 million pounds of their giardiniera, and they also supply 35 private label customers, including Aldi and Jewel.

At Al's #1, Chris Pacelli believes that they were serving "hot peppers" on their beef sandwiches since the day they opened.

As is evident, the exact origins of Chicago-style giardiniera are, as with so many foods, exceedingly difficult to determine with 100 percent accuracy.

There is also no definitive recipe for giardiniera. Look through a random selection of different giardiniera varieties at an Italian market in the Chicagoland area, and you'll find that certain ingredients seem to predominate in bottles from different manufacturers. Sometimes, as with Serrelli's house brand, hot chili peppers predominate; in other brands, there are olives. This olive-forward variety of giardiniera is what's used on the muffuletta, a famous and much beloved meat and cheese sandwich served on trademark round bread, developed by the Sicilian American owner of New Orleans' Central Grocery.

WHERE TO GET GIARDINIERA

At a Chicago Italian beef stand, it's guaranteed that if you ask for your sandwich "hot," you will get giardiniera. You can buy many brands of giardiniera online at Amazon; at many Chicagoland grocery stores, like Jewel; or at Italian grocery stores such as the following.

Serrelli's Finer Foods
6454 W. North Avenue
773-237-7530

J. P. Graziano Grocery
901 W. Randolph
312-666-4587

Freddy's Pizza
1600 S. 61st Street, Cicero
708-863-9389

HOW TO MAKE GIARDINIERA AT HOME

Ingredients

- 2 cups water
- ¼ cup kosher salt
- 1 cup carrots, diced small
- 1 cup tiny cauliflower florets (crumble larger clusters as necessary)
- 4 to 8 serrano peppers, sliced (depending on the desired level of heat)
- 2 cloves garlic, minced
- 1 stalk celery, diced small
- 1 red bell pepper, diced small
- 2 cups canola oil (canola oil is standard, but you can use olive oil)
- 1 tablespoon dried oregano
- ½ teaspoon freshly ground black pepper

Procedure

1. Combine water and salt in a glass or other non-reactive bowl. Mix until the salt is dissolved.
2. Add carrots, cauliflower, serranos, garlic, celery, and bell pepper to the salted water and stir to combine. Cover and refrigerate overnight.
3. Next day, drain and rinse the vegetables.
4. In a bowl, mix the oil with the oregano and pepper. Add the vegetables and mix to combine. Allow to marinate overnight.
5. After about 2 days in the bowl, place the mixture in airtight mason jars. Refrigerated, the giardiniera will keep for at least 2 to 3 weeks.

13

GAM PONG CHICKEN WINGS

Monica Eng

SAUCY CHICKEN WING LOLLIPOPS

Gam pong chicken wings. Photo: Monica Eng

It's hard to choose the best part of this classic Chicago dish.

Is it the initial garlic and umami aroma? The crisp, juicy chicken smooshed to one end of the bone? Or the sweet, fiery sauce that lingers on your tongue and radiates heat up through your head?

The answer, like the dish itself, is complicated.

So, it's fitting that gam pong gi (or lollipop) chicken wings took such a complicated journey to Chicago—one driven by floods, famine, drought, migration, biased property laws, crazy-low wing prices, America's love of sweetness, and finally, a need to be tidy.

But let's start at the beginning.

A dish called gam pong gi has long been a staple of a certain kind of eatery known (by me) as Chinese Korean restaurants. Started in Korea in the twentieth century, these restaurants are now scattered throughout Asia and the Americas, but they're fading.

The restaurants were first launched by Chinese immigrants who arrived in Korea during the early part of the twentieth century from the northern Chinese province of Shandong. Tens of thousands immigrated to flee floods, famine, and unemployment in their region and to find new opportunities in Korea.

Many became merchants or opened restaurants serving Shandong style Chinese food that was eventually modified to suit Korean tastes. These modifications often meant using more red pepper powder, certain types of fermented foods, or just serving side dishes of sweet daikon pickles and kimchi.

While early Chinese American restaurants became known for egg rolls, fried rice, and chop suey, these Chinese Korean restaurants in Korea were famous for jajangmyun (noodles in brown gravy), tansuyuk (sweet and sour pork) and jjampong (a spicy red seafood noodle soup)—and also gam pong gi, a spicy fried chicken dish using the whole chicken, the launching pad from which Chicago's wings would eventually take flight.

That flight wouldn't happen, though, until Chinese Korean restaurants arrived in the United States in the latter half of the twentieth century, prompted by changing laws that put Chinese immigrants in Korea at a disadvantage.

CHINESE IMMIGRANTS LEAVE KOREA

Frank Wang was part of an early wave of Chinese who left Korea for other countries in the Americas and Taiwan. He said many Chinese prospered in Korean Chinatowns as merchants in the first half of the twentieth century.

"But after World War II, things changed," explained Wang, who left Korea in the 1960s. "At that time, a lot of us moved from North Korea to South and the [South Korean Government] started to discriminate against the Chinese immigrants. We could not even own a property. If you wanted property you would have to have a Korean take the title and you rented from them.

"And the only business license you could get was essentially just a restaurant license," Wang continued. "The others were very hard. So many of us moved to Taiwan or South America. And some of us, like me, moved to the United States."

Wang was part of one of the earliest groups of these Chinese emigres that went from Korea to the United States. Many would follow in the 1970s and '80s, settling on the East Coast, West Coast, and in Chicago. Here they moved into neighborhoods on the Northwest Side, especially in Korean areas around Albany Park, Lincolnwood, and Ravenswood.

Their restaurants often looked like typical Chinese American eateries, but sometimes featured the words "Mandarin" or "Peking" or "Beijing" in their names and descriptions. This small detail set them apart from most Chinese restaurants in the United States at the time, which were run by Cantonese Chinese and focused on Southern Chinese cuisine.

Korean Americans flocked to these distinctive restaurants, which served familiar Chinese Korean dishes, for a taste of home. The ethnically Chinese proprietors would speak Korean to these customers and serve them bright yellow daikon pickles as well as turnip kimchi with their meals.

But to the average Chicagoan, the places just looked like Chinese restaurants where—if you paid attention—many Korean people tended to eat.

GAM PONG GI MAKES ITS WAY TO CHICAGO

Like their counterparts back in Korea, these restaurants were known for four main dishes: noodles in brown sauce, sweet and sour pork, spicy seafood soup, and a fried chicken dish called gam pong gi. But that chicken dish looked a lot different than it does today.

"[Gam pong gi] was basically a whole chicken cut up into eight pieces," says Frank Wang, who would end up owning two Chinese Korean restaurants in the United States. "In Korea we actually called it 'chop eight whole chicken' instead of gam pong gi, because people said, 'I want eight pieces of chicken—two each of breast, thigh, legs, and wings.'"

Roger Kao, who owns the Chinese Korean restaurant Great Beijing in Lincolnwood, Illinois, concurs. But in the early 1980s, he says the gam pong gi served in Chicago started to change, thanks to two ethnically Chinese Korean chefs. One of them was Kao's now-retired uncle Hsing-Tseng Kao, who opened Peking Mandarin restaurant in Albany Park in 1983.

There, Kao says, his uncle Hsing-Tseng had been cooking that traditional Shandong-style gam pong gi dish using a whole chopped bird tossed with hot chilis, ginger and garlic, as Wang described.

But in the early 1980s, he got an idea from the ultra-cheap prices he saw for American chicken wings. The Chinese had long prized chicken wings as one of the tastiest parts of the bird, and Kao was astonished to find that they were considered a trash cut, and sometimes even thrown away.

"This was in 1983, and my uncle thought this was too waste-y," Roger Kao told me for a WBEZ story. "So, he started to find something to not waste this part and he created these [wings]."

But just a few blocks away (also on Lawrence Avenue), another Chinese Korean restaurant called Great Sea also started making gam pong gi with wings.

And as Jennifer Tiao tells it, her father Nai Tiao came up with an innovation to improve the recipe further.

"Gam pong gi wings were originally supposed to be dry and served fried with no sauce [although some recipes do include a little sauce]," Tiao says. "But my dad was like, 'The sauce is so good. Why not make a whole bunch of it so you can dip it in and eat it?'"

So, chef Nai Tiao bathed his gam pong gi wings in a delicious house-made sauce that balanced the original heat of the dish with a pronounced sweetness for the American palate. Customers liked it so much that the restaurant started bottling it and selling it at the checkout counter.

Still, there was just one problem: this sweet, sticky sauce made the dish extremely messy to eat. But that only gave chef Nai another idea: to create a lollipop handle (called frenching in the chef world) on each wing stick.

"My mom and dad loved eating wings," Jennifer Tiao explained for a 2017 WBEZ story. "But my dad wanted to make it cleaner and easier. So, he did that by pushing all the meat down on the bone, so you have a kind of handle."

Frenching those wings to get that handle, she says, is a pain in the neck and requires three steps. "We'd break two parts of the joint, and then cut each section of the wing, and then the tip is thrown out," Tiao said.

This process was so laborious that when Jennifer and her sister, Karen Lim, opened their own place called Take Me Out in Pilsen (with lollipop wings as their star attraction), they dispensed with the frenching, thinking they could get away with it. But customer demand forced them to bring the frenching back.

While many continue to go through the trouble of frenching their wings, most do not. And frankly, the dish requires a lot of napkins either way.

In 2017, Great Sea was purchased from the Tiao family by Frank Wang—who got the secret recipe for the sauce and wings in the deal. Great Sea has since been acquired by another owner, and the Tiao daughters have also since sold their "wingporium" in Pilsen.

But the latest owners tell me that the dish remains a top seller at Great Seas, Peking Mandarin, Great Beijing, and many spots beyond, where it has landed to tantalize local tastebuds.

WHERE TO GET GAM PONG CHICKEN WINGS

Great Sea Restaurant
3253 W Lawrence Ave.
773-478-9129

Joong Boo Market
3333 N Kimball Ave.
773-478-5566

Great Beijing Restaurant
6717 N Lincoln Ave.
Lincolnwood
847-673-5588

Peking Mandarin Restaurant
3459 W Lawrence Ave
773-478-5338

GYROS

Monica Eng

SEASONED AND GROUND MEAT, CUT FROM A SPIT AND SERVED WITH PITA BREAD

Gyros sandwich. Photo: Monica Eng

Fragrant cones of seasoned meat spin in restaurants and food stalls all over the world. Think shawarma in the Middle East, tacos al pastor in Mexico, doner in Turkey, and gyros in Greece.

Each of these vertical rotisserie treats offer considerable charm, but none has seeped so deep and wide into the far corners of American food culture as gyros.

For that we can thank the ingenuity of Greek American innovators who came to Chicago in the 1960s and played key roles in bringing this Greek-ish food to the masses.

So, just to set expectations straight, this is not a story of how gyros was invented. For that, you'd need to go back to the nineteenth-century Ottoman Empire or, some even suggest, to Alexander the Great. But it's believed that gyros traveled to Greece from Turkey (where it was called doner) through refugees who arrived in Greece from Istanbul in the early part of the twentieth century. Eventually, Greeks brought it to the United States.

This chapter is about how those Greek Americans created mass-market gyros in Chicago and then spread it across the country and beyond.

WHAT'S GYROS?

The name "gyros" is derived from a Greek word that means "to turn"—and in Greece that turning meat is usually whole muscle chunks of seasoned pork. But when Greek Americans brought the concept to beef-loving Chicago, that recipe changed quickly from pork to beef or beef mixed with lamb, according to Peter Parthenis Jr. of Grecian Delight Foods.

This mixture of ground beef and lamb plays a starring role in many Chicago fast foods, but the first and most popular is the classic gyros sandwich.

It all starts with warm, pliable, Greek pita bread, which is different from Middle Eastern pita that features a pocket. Ideally, the pita should come off the hot griddle moments before the sandwich is assembled, starting with hot, juicy strips of gyros meat sporting crispy, browned edges. Next come fat ripe tomato wedges, pungent white onion slices, and a nice plop of cooling tzatziki made with cucumbers, yogurt (sometimes sour cream), garlic, and mint.

If you're in Chicago, this will most likely be delivered in a plastic basket lined with deli paper and some golden thick-cut fries. As you stare at your sandwich, trying to figure out the least awkward way to pick it up, you'll take in the aroma of roasted meat, raw onions, garlic, and oregano.

And you will definitely start to salivate.

As you grab the sandwich for your first bite, expect condiments and meat to start spilling out—that's what the basket is for. But by the second bite you won't mind because you'll be too busy enjoying this chewy, savory, creamy, sharp, oozy, and meaty delight to notice.

High-quality supporting ingredients do play a role in making the sandwich work. But I'll be honest with you: I've had Chicago gyros sandwiches where the pita was stale, the tomatoes were less than ripe, the onions too sharp, and the tzatziki skimpy—but I still ate the whole dang thing, with gusto! And that, I believe, is a testament to the consistent, near foolproof "meat product" invented in Chicago in the early 1970s: the unified, preformed, mass-produced gyros cone.

HOW CHICAGO SENT GYROS SPINNING AROUND THE COUNTRY

The years between 1965 and 1975 saw such a flurry of gyros activity in Chicago that it's hard to tell exactly which Greek American is most responsible for what we know as gyros across the country. The fairest way to describe it would probably be as a group effort with some serving it in restaurants, others building rotisserie machines, and others mass-producing versions to ship all over the country. The following account is, like a gyros cone itself, a spicy, delicious mixture of many elements that form a tasty whole.

Cones of ground spiced meat were being roasted and sliced into sandwiches in Chicago as early as the mid-'60s according to Chicago area gyros maker Devanco Foods, which says its founder, George Apostolou, served the first U.S. gyros at his Parkview Restaurant in 1965. This fits in with an account from Peter Parthenis Sr. of Grecian Delight Foods, who told me he spotted the spit-roasted meat in Chicago restaurants shortly after he arrived from Greece as an engineering student in 1964.

By late 1968, Chris Liakouras says he started serving gyros at the Parthenon in Greektown, where, he told Michael Nagrant of the *Chicago Tribune's* RedEye edition, he gave away free samples to introduce his customers to the food.

One of those customers was the *Chicago Tribune's* Kay Loring, who wrote about enjoying gyros at the Parthenon in April of 1969. Later, in June 1969, she described another version she tried at the Olympic Flame in Lincoln Square: "Before we left, the chef sliced off a bit of what he called gyros for us to sample—a great round meat cake resembling meatloaf being broiled on another large spit. The mixture consisted of ground lamb, beef, onions, parsley etc. bound together with eggs. It was delicious."

Although the Parthenon famously stacked its gyros using whole muscle pieces of meat, Parthenis says most restaurant gyros cones at the time were made using ground meat, like the one described above.

Unfortunately, those cones were usually cooked using wonky rotisserie machines made in Greece that frequently broke down and needed new parts. This was a pain for restaurant operators, but ended up giving Parthenis, an engineering student at the University of Illinois at Chicago in the late 1960s, an idea. "Being fresh Greek I wanted the Greek food I was used to, so I would go to the Greek restaurants on Halsted for lunch and I got to know the owners," he recalled. "One day they told me 'you're an engineer . . . can you find some parts for the rotisseries to cook the gyros?'"

As Parthenis helped them fix and find parts for their finicky machines, it dawned on him that he should design one that he could build right in Chicago. He says it took him a few years of tinkering in his Lincoln Square basement to finally come up with a finished product. But by the early 1970s he'd finally perfected a gyros rotisserie and started shopping it around.

Peter Parthenis Sr. at the National Restaurant Show in Chicago, circa early 1970s. Courtesy of Grecian Delight Foods

Still, while he was out on sales calls—during which he would also teach restaurateurs how to make their own gyros cones—he had a new epiphany.

"Basically, I realized what IBM realized," he said. "They were trying to make money with hardware, and they gave away the software to Bill Gates. But the money was not in the hardware, it was in the software."

So instead of continuing to make and sell the rotisserie [the hardware], which could last for ten years or more, he wanted to start making and selling the meat [the software], "because it repeats every week with another order and then another order."

Around the same time, Chicago's Papantoniou brothers were working on mass producing gyros cones at Olympic Gyros, after originally starting their business as a pita bread–baking operation. And by 1975, Chris Tomaros at Kronos Gyros (a company that would merge with Grecian Delight in 2020) was also making what Kronos calls the "first" preformed gyro cones.

Initially, Parthenis said he considered getting into the gyros cone business by working with existing Chicago meat companies, "but they didn't want to because there was too much work involved and the market was too small."

Then, around 1974, he said he found a small gyros company in Milwaukee called Gyros Inc., run by former Marine and Cadillac salesman John Garlic along with his wife Margaret. (The Garlics would later open a restaurant featuring live dolphin shows in Milwaukee; I am not kidding). At first, Parthenis says, he worked with the couple as partners.

"But they were not promoting it enough or properly, so I bought [the company] and started with a two thousand square foot kitchen in Skokie in 1974," he recalls.

At the time, the process wasn't automated, and it took a worker twenty-five minutes to make a single cone.

"In the old days we used to take chunks of this mixed, sticky meat, put it on a table, and a strong employee with strong muscles would make hamburger patty shapes—but thick—and stick them through the skewer and stack them up," he recalled. "And as you go higher the diameter of those patties . . . would be larger and larger, and that is how you would make the cone. Then to make it smooth, you would take a knife and cut all around . . . And to do that you needed a lot of muscle and time."

So Parthenis says he brainstormed a way to make the whole thing more efficient.

"I got the machine you use to stuff sausages and I filled a cylindrical can under pressure. Then I put this cylindrical meat on an angle on a band saw and trimmed it to make a perfect cone and that process would take two to three minutes."

Today, shipping is done on refrigerated trailer trucks, but in the early days, he says, they had less sophisticated methods.

"While I was [at the first plant in] Skokie, we used to send the product out of the state on Greyhound buses solid frozen," he says. "I used to take some of the boxes in my car and load it up and go to the Greyhound station. A restaurant in Atlanta was our first out-of-state customer."

Now that he'd perfected a way to quickly make the cones and freeze them, he'd have to figure out how to get restaurants to use them instead of making their own. He said he zeroed in on the issues of safety and time.

"They used to make the product in their heated restaurant kitchen that were not as cold and sanitary as our facilities," he said. "They also realized that it took too much time and work, and the labor force was getting tight for specialists in this field who knew what they were doing."

But he says he also sold them on the juicy profits they could make, using a slogan that went something like "Gyros lets you 'turn' a profit."

He explained that gyros could deliver "three times the hot dog profit and two times the hamburger profit," he said. "But the truth is that the gyros sandwich is a very tasty, hand carved, hot and juicy sandwich."

As Parthenis continued to market his product, he said he got an idea from a natural gas salesperson (Parthenis's rotisseries were heated by gas) who urged him to debut the machine and cones at the National Restaurant Association show in Chicago—"sometime in the mid-1970s."

"It was the first time we went to the restaurant show and then that exploded because the whole of America saw the concept of the sandwich," he said. "We served gyros as a sample with toothpicks, and we had long lines. Every hour the management of the show would come and stop us because the lines were too long. That was fun!"

The meat was advertised at the show with the sign: "New European food sensation Gyros is here."

"One year when we were at the National Restaurant Association show, the people from the Chicago Hilton came and they said, 'We want this product to have for weddings in our buffet,'" Parthenis recalled. "And we used that as a marketing tool selling to restaurants, because Hilton gave credence and prestige to the sandwich."

By the late 1970s, Parthenis says, gyros had spread out to most major cities in the United States, and it has only grown from there.

As a testament to Chicago's centrality in the gyros cone market, many of the biggest manufacturers still have their headquarters in the area. A few have been acquired by nearby competitors who have expanded to a wider array of Mediterranean foods and even plant-based proteins, including vegan gyros. Some of the biggest names left standing include Devanco, Olympic, and Grecian Delight, which merged with Kronos in 2020.

Today in Chicago, you can find gyros incorporated into dozens of local dishes, including burgers, Pizza Puffs (chapter 10), specialty fries, Jim Shoes (chapter 17), salads, and pizza toppings.

When I ask Parthenis if he is surprised that gyros has found its way into so many different places and foods, he laughs.

"That is what we did years ago in our marketing," he said. "We promoted different ways to use gyros. Put it on top of a salad, put it on top of a cheeseburger, put it on top of an omelet instead of sausage. We made beautiful brochures telling people to do this, so I am not surprised."

So even if the actual invention of gyros was a group effort involving Alexander the Great, some Turks, and other notable (Chicago area) Greeks, Parthenis is pleased to have had a part in "turning on" more people to it around the country and the world.

Today, his son, Peter Parthenis Jr., runs the much-expanded company based in suburban Elk Grove Village, Illinois, while his dad enjoys life.

"We did a lot of hard work and had fun with it," he says, "and, in the end, we're very successful, thank God."

WHERE TO GET GYROS

Hubs
5540 N. Lincoln Ave.
773-784-4240

Mr. Gyros
234 S. Halsted St.
(312) 906-8731

Athenian Room
807 W. Webster Ave.
773-348-5155

Central Gyros
3127 N. Central Ave.
773-545-1276

PS: You can also buy whole Kronos gyros kits with meat, bread, and tzatziki included in many local grocery stores.

ITALIAN BEEF SANDWICH

David Hammond

THIN SLICED BEEF IN *JUS*, SPICED WITH OREGANO AND GARLIC, TOPPED WITH SWEET PEPPERS, GIARDINIERA, OR BOTH, SERVED ON A WHITE FLOUR ROLL

Al's #1 Italian Beef. Photo: David Hammond

It sometimes seems a great surprise to Chicagoans that few people outside the metro area have ever heard of Italian beef. It's probably equally surprising that once a Chicagoan starts explaining the Italian beef to non-Chicagoans, the response is usually a questioning look that says, "That's it? What's the big deal?"

Truth be told, the Italian beef is a remarkably simple sandwich: thin-sliced meat, frequently drenched in a *jus* of oregano, garlic, and other spices, topped with sweet peppers, giardiniera (chapter 12), or both, and served on a white flour roll. Some refer to the roll as "Italian bread," though Turano, as well as other top local bread providers like Gonnella, label those rolls "French bread." Suffice to say the roll used for an Italian beef is pretty much the same kind of roll used for submarine sandwiches at most Italian delis and specialty stores. The word "roll," however, may be a little misleading, as the bread used for Italian beef is many times cut from a longer, baguette-type loaf.

The beef, the *jus*, and the French bread may suggest that the Italian beef is a variation on the French dip sandwich, but there are several competing theories as to the origin of the Chicago Italian beef.

WHO MADE THE FIRST ITALIAN BEEF?

Italian beef has sometimes been served outside Chicago, in places like New York and Los Angeles. Still, the first recorded appearance of the sandwich was in Chicago. What's more in dispute is where in Chicago—and how—this sandwich originated. There are two well-known commercial contenders for the title of being "the place where Italian beef was invented": Al's #1 Italian Beef and Scala Packing Company.

At the website for Al's #1 Italian Beef, it's explained that "In 1938, Al Ferreri and his sister and brother-in-law, Frances and Chris Pacelli Sr., opened up a little family beef stand located in the Little Italy neighborhood on Harrison and Laflin Streets."

Recently, we caught up with Chris Pacelli Jr. on the phone as he was making a delivery, still working hard to retain Al's position as a major Italian beef joint in Chicago.

Here's his explanation of the origin of Al's: "You got to remember Italians, in the 1930s, late 20s, there were all kinds of gamblers, half-assed Mafia guys and stuff. My uncle Al was involved in all that, a gambler, dis dat. Well, he gets in trouble, has to go to jail, comes out of jail, and starts driving a truck. A friend says, 'Let's open up a bookie place.' So, my uncle says, 'Why don't I do beef sandwiches? I'll sell them as a front.' There was like five guys. The original beef stand was on Laflin and Harrison. They didn't have gas or nothing in those days, so everything was charcoal. First name for this idea was 'Al's Barbecue.'

"Couple of years go by," says Pacelli, "and my uncle is thinking, 'I'm pretty good at this, and I don't want to jeopardize it all by going to jail because I'm operating a bookie joint,' so he talks to the guys and says, 'I want to buy you out.' So, he pays them what they wanted and hires a couple of people.

"My father at the time was working for what they called 'the streetcar company'—now it's the CTA—and my mother was a maid, cleaning houses for doctors and attorneys. So, my uncle says, 'Why don't you come work for me?' He was driving a truck during the day. Now, they're all working during the day and what they'd do is open up at night. They called the place Baba's at first, because that was my Uncle's nickname. We all had nicknames; mine's Bones; you come to my neighborhood and ask for Chris, no one's going to know who the hell you're looking for; you have to ask for Bonesy. We're a neighborhood of nicknames.

"So, this went on until the late 1950s, and a lot of these beef places—like Carm's and Mr. Beef—they all started out because of gambling. Scala didn't start doing Italian beef until 1960, '61. We bought the raw product from them. All these beef stands started because of my uncle. They were gamblers, and they saw him making money, cash money, and they figured that's an easy way to make money and still gamble. They needed a source of money and instead of stealing, they sold beef."

That's one story about the origin of the Italian beef. Here's another.

According to the Facebook page for what is now called Scala's Preferred Italian Beef and Sausage, "It all began just after the end of World War I, in the old Lucca Bakery on South Western Avenue, in the heart of one of Chicago's Italian neighborhoods . . . when the Great Depression arrived, times were hard and 'necessity became the mother of invention.' At a time when food and other goods were scarce, Scala Packing helped develop and introduce the concept of serving thinly sliced beef on a bun and loaded with gravy. This meal was originally introduced at weddings and banquets where the meat was sliced thinly so there would be enough to feed all the guests. It rapidly grew in popularity and eventually became Chicago's most famous ethnic food: the original Italian Beef."

The Chicago Food Encyclopedia suggests yet a third, noncommercial origin story, speculating that "though some businesses claim to have invented Italian Beef (Al's, Scala), its unique origins clearly lie in Italian-American cooking. The key stage in the development of the sandwich was its use in so-called 'peanut weddings' (attested from the 1920s). Working-class Italian families would rent halls and supply their own food for the event, commonly including roasted peanuts and sandwiches filled with slices of wet-roasted beef . . . Similar weddings were common elsewhere (New York's Italian 'football weddings' with sub sandwiches), but beef sandwiches are specific to Chicago."

ORDERING PROTOCOL AND "THE STANCE"

As you might expect, there are many variations on the basic Italian beef sandwich. For instance, the "combo" adds an Italian sausage to the beef and serves them together in a bun. Sometimes cheese may be added to the Italian beef, or the whole sandwich may be served on a croissant. As you might expect, longtime Chicagoans do not always countenance such variations.

An "Italian soaker" or "gravy bread" is simply the bread used for the Italian beef sandwich without meat but drenched in *jus*, very satisfying if admittedly not very substantial. This is food of desperation, food of the Great Depression, much like the french fry sandwich one sees at some Chicago barbecue joints, the kind of thing you might eat when you have no money for meat. Still, if you order a quantity of beef and bread to make the sandwiches at home, you'll probably have some *jus* and bread left over . . . and there's no shame in enjoying gravy bread. It's tasty.

When ordering an Italian beef with lots of flavor and taste dimension, I ask for it "dipped" or "wet" (soaked in *jus*) and "sweet and hot," which is a pleasing combination of sweet green peppers and giardiniera (chapter 12), the Chicago-style mixture of chilies and other vegetables in oil.

At Al's and other beef stands, you'll see guys with their recently purchased Italian beef sandwiches stand at the counter, unfold the thin white paper around the sandwich, and assume "the stance." This position has the diner standing with his or her feet about a foot or so apart, waist back, arms bent with elbows on the counter, leaning over the sandwich. This posture is intended to minimize beef drippings on the front of your shirt. Also called the "Italian stance," this is a Chicago ritual, like the very vocal, ritualistic put-downs of those who ask for ketchup on their hot dog, a city-specific sin tantamount to parking in a space upon which someone else has already called "dibs."

On Taylor Street in Chicago's Little Italy, Al's Beef is located across the street from Mario's Italian Lemonade. The combination of slightly spicy beef and cool, sweet Italian ice is a winner. At places like the justly renowned Johnnie's Beef in Elmwood Park, Italian ice is served right along with the Italian beef sandwiches, and they are, indeed, a satisfying one-two punch.

WHO MAKES THE BEST ITALIAN BEEF?

Al's #1 Italian Beef and Johnnie's Beef head up most lists of the best Italian beef sandwiches in the Chicago area. Every place processes their meat differently (some ship it in, ready to just heat up and serve, and other places like Al's #1 season, cook, and slice their meat in house). And many places have their own spicing for the *jus* and giardiniera. Having done side-by-side tastings at dozens of Italian beef places in the Chicago area, I can say with assurance that there are differences, sometimes quite noticeable, among the Italian beef sandwiches that are served at restaurants and street-side stands in Chicago.

WHERE TO GET ITALIAN BEEF

Al's #1 Italian Beef
1079 W. Taylor, and other
locations throughout Chicago

Johnnie's Beef
7500 W. North Ave.,
Elmwood Park
708-452-6000

Mr. Beef On Orleans
666 N. Orleans
312-337-8500

16

JIBARITO

Monica Eng

A "SANDWICH" OF CRISP FRIED PLANTAINS FILLED WITH JUICY MEAT, TOMATO, AND CHEESE

Jibarito sandwich. Photo: Monica Eng

Some Puerto Ricans might take offense at the term *jibaro* (HEE-bah-roh), which means hillbilly in Puerto Rican slang. But Juan C. Figueroa sees it as a badge of honor.

"I am a jibaro," he told me over coffee one morning. "I am a hillbilly from Puerto Rico. I am from the mountains and that is what jibaros are."

Thanks to Figueroa, the name—especially the diminutive jibarito—has also become synonymous with one of the most delectable sandwiches ever birthed in Chicago.

WHAT'S IN A JIBARITO?

Like so many Chicago sandwiches, the jibarito offers a novel riff on a classic steak sandwich, but with its own unique deliciousness.

Inside the sandwich you find mayonnaise, cheese, thin seared steak, tomato, and lettuce. But what makes the jibarito different is its outer casing: crisp, fragrant, fried plantains that take the place of bread.

Puerto Rican cuisine features lots of starchy fried green plantains in dishes like mofongo (fried plantain, mashed and sometimes pressed into balls) and tostones (plantains cut up, smashed into discs, and fried). But the jibarito takes that tradition a step further by cutting the green plantain lengthwise, and then flattening and frying each slice to make top and bottom "buns."

And while steak filled the first iteration of a jibarito, these days you can find chicken, ham, roast pork, blood sausage, seafood, and even vegetable versions of the sandwich. If you're really lucky, the restaurant will top the whole thing off with a shmear of garlicky oil, adding a final, perfect flourish to the sandwich.

HOW DID THE JIBARITO COME ABOUT?

Well, it almost didn't. When Figueroa came to the United States from Jajuya, Puerto Rico, in the late 1970s, he recalls overseeing a string of flopped businesses, despite financial help from his father.

"I was young, and I didn't want to work hard," he said. "I just wanted to have fun. So, I failed a bunch of times."

But then one day in 1996, Figueroa was sitting in his most recent anemic business—a tiny storefront restaurant on California Avenue in Humboldt Park called Borinquen—when he read an article that would change his life.

"I was reading this newspaper from Puerto Rico called 'El Vocero,' the voice of the people," Figueroa told me in 2003, for a story I was writing for the *Chicago Tribune*. "I used to buy the newspaper from Puerto Rico every day so I could have something to do while I waited for the customers. And the first thing I would always do is go to the recipe page. So, I came across this recipe for something called *sandwich de platano* (plantain sandwich). I didn't have nothing else to do, so I went into the kitchen and made it."

Figueroa peeled, sliced, fried, and flattened the green plantains then assembled the "sandwich" with steak, mayonnaise, and American cheese.

He says he marched out to the dining room to find his dad, and "I told my father, 'Father, eat this sandwich.'"

Figueroa senior was blown away by his son's sandwich and asked for one every day. Before the elder Figueroa left for his annual jaunt to Puerto Rico that year, he urged his son to put it on the menu.

"When he got back from vacation, I was already selling more than 100 a day," Figueroa recalled. "And soon people started flocking to the restaurant, lots of people. And I kept hiring new people and teaching them how to make it. And all the sudden, I'm in the middle of the scene."

That scene unfolded in the middle of Chicago's Puerto Rican community around Humboldt Park. But it didn't take long for word to travel and for competitors to start sniffing around.

"After about six or seven months, owners of other restaurants would come and camp outside my restaurant just to see what kind of flow we had," Figueroa told me in 2003. "Then they would send people in to buy the sandwiches so they could try and copy them."

Those imitators have now spread across the region with several restaurants that even use the word "jibarito" in their names.

Figueroa said his brother, Angel, even suggested that he patent the sandwich.

So, what's the secret to its popularity?

"It's about layers of flavor," Figueroa said, "the crispy plantain, the juicy meat, the cool tomato and the cheese."

When these layers of flavors come together, they create an irresistible combination of tastes, temperatures, and textures. But they also make the sandwich tricky to eat without parts—the meat, the tomato, the cheese—squishing out the other end.

My best advice is to use a fork and knife when possible and to eat it just moments after it's served. Like french fries, fried plantains start to lose that crisp-on-the-outside-soft-on-the-inside magic shortly after emerging from the fryer.

So, don't let that takeout order sit in the bag too long. Go ahead and eat it in your parked car, if you must. Just remember to grab a lot of napkins.

SISTER SANDWICHES

Back in the 1990s, Figueroa created a sister sandwich to the jibarito called the jibarita. It swaps in cooked ripe plantains for the green starchy ones to make a sweet and savory dish that must be eaten with fork and knife. You can find it at the newly remodeled Borinquen Lounge on Western Avenue, which is owned by Figueroa's brother, Angel.

Today, Figueroa is retired, but before he got out of the restaurant business, he told me about yet another idea: to make breakfast jibaritos with eggs and ham between the plantains. Unsurprisingly, those too have popped up on Chicago menus, including at Nellie's, a Puerto Rican diner on Division Street.

WHERE TO GET A JIBARITO

Not long after the sandwich took off in Chicago it was also picked up by Puerto Rican restaurants in Cleveland and Milwaukee. These days you can also find it in New York City, New Jersey, and Philadelphia. But strangely enough, the sandwich still has no big presence in Puerto Rico. Figueroa said his father tried to open a jibarito restaurant in Puerto Rico years ago, but it never really took off. There is, however, at least one restaurant on the island that serves a sandwich de platano.

Today you can find the sandwich in dozens of locations all over the Chicago area. Here are a few of the best.

Jibaritos Y Mas
3400 W. Fullerton Ave.
773-799-8601

Borinquen Lounge
3811 N. Western Ave.
773-442-8001

Jibaritos on Harlem
3317 N Harlem Ave.
773-647-1122

JIM SHOE

Monica Eng

CORNED BEEF, ROAST BEEF, AND GYROS MEAT ON A SUBMARINE ROLL, TOPPED WITH GIARDINIERA, TOMATOES, LETTUCE, ONIONS, MAYONNAISE, CHEESE, AND A LIQUID-Y APPROXIMATION OF TZATZIKI

Jim Shoe sandwich with fries. Photo: Monica Eng

The freeway of Chicago delicacies is littered with many cultural collisions, but few match the complexity of a culinary ten-car pileup known as the Jim Shoe.

Drawing influences from Greek, Italian, Jewish, African American, Pakistani, Palestinian/Jordanian, Mexican, and even stoner culture, the Jim Shoe's origin remains up for grabs more than thirty years after the sandwich jogged onto Chicago fast-food menu boards.

That's not to say that people aren't willing to offer origin stories—it's just that none of them feel particularly definitive. In the end, it may be that the original "Jim" just never bothered to claim credit for this unique creation.

If the sandwich has an analog in the United States, it might be the Rochester "garbage plate" featuring home fries and macaroni salad topped with hot dogs and hamburgers slathered in meat sauce and chopped onions—you know, stuff that's already hanging around a diner kitchen just waiting to be mushed together.

With all due respect to Rochester, I tend to prefer our own culinary mash-up, a dish with flavors as bold as the origin stories it has inspired.

WHAT'S IN A JIM SHOE?

Like a lot of the delicacies in this book, most Jim Shoes are cranked out by cooks at independent fast-food shops—often called sub shops—in African American neighborhoods of Chicago's South and West Sides.

Owned primarily by Middle Eastern and South Asian entrepreneurs, these spots crop up in areas ignored or underserved by big chains. And this independent ownership, by mostly Muslims, produces two interesting things: nearly porkless menus that don't seem to bother anyone, and a freedom to create new customer-pleasing combos on the spot—or copy and riff on ones your neighbor makes. This helps explain not only the creation of the Jim Shoe but also the variations you see from one shop to another.

That said, most Jim Shoes feature the following: corned beef, roast beef, and gyros meat on a submarine roll, topped with giardiniera, tomatoes, lettuce, onions, mayonnaise, cheese, and a liquid-y approximation of tzatziki, locally called guy-roh sauce.

The original Jim Shoe appears to have been a cold affair, with layered slices of the three meats in a submarine sandwich—yes, cool gyros, yuck. That is the way Stony Sub co-owner Mo Al-Masri and Southtown Sub manager Abdul Wajid Khan say they were first introduced to the sandwich.

Still, both have long since pivoted to the much tastier hot Jim Shoe. This version chops and fries the meat, giardiniera peppers, and onions on the griddle until the flavors meld into a pile of crispy-edged deliciousness.

Further permutations of the hot Jim Shoe include the Super Jim Shoe taco. It features the fillings cradled in toasted pita bread instead of a sub roll—somewhat reminiscent of tacos al arabe, served in Puebla Mexico. You can also find a halal Jim Shoe—free of any prohibited ingredients—in Chicago's Albany Park.

And finally, there is the super crispy Jim Shoe, a delicacy you can special order at some skillful, but not too busy, Jim Shoe-terias. This creation features all the griddled Jim Shoe ingredients wrapped up in a giant flour tortilla, sealed up and then lowered gingerly into a deep fryer. If it doesn't explode and spoil the oil, it emerges as the biggest, most flavor-packed egg roll thing you've ever eaten. I'm not going to guarantee this was influenced by the Chinese, but well . . . if the Jim Shoe fits.

WHERE DID IT COME FROM?

Dr. Peter Engler, a South Side food historian and a genetic researcher by training, has been trying to track down the source of the Jim Shoe for decades. And while he's found lots of solid meals in the process, he's found very few solid origin stories.

One day, though, he thought he'd finally hit pay dirt while interviewing yet another sub shop owner through the bulletproof glass you find in many of these spots. As they were talking through the possible Jim Shoe origins, the owner's assistant came up to the window claiming he had the answer.

"At last, I thought, my quest will be over," Engler recalled in a 2013 post on LTHForum.com. "[Just then the assistant] pointed to his head and announced dramatically: 'It comes from the mind.'"

THE STONER THEORY

Slightly more convincing was the explanation I got from a Jordanian-born fast-food entrepreneur. I was interviewing him in 2018 for a story about his invention of Chicago's steak and lemonade combo when he told me that *he* had, in fact, invented the Jim Shoe. He claimed it was inspired by a specific request from an intoxicated customer.

"One late night [around 2006] this guy who was high on weed came to my drive thru window," he said. "When I asked him for his order, he told me, 'I don't care man. I just need something with a lot of meats on it right now.' So, I said, 'how about if I just drop a whole bunch of meat on a gym shoe and serve that to you? Would you eat that?' He said, 'Sure, man, that would be great.' So, I made him a sandwich with roast beef, corned beef and gyros meat and I called it a Jim Shoe."

It's a terrific story and it illustrates the ease with which Jim Shoes can be made with existing South Side fast-food shop ingredients. I might have even entertained the theory if there were not credible Jim Shoe sightings in Chicago several years before that period.

FAR SOUTH SIDE THEORY

Engler said he'd personally seen the sandwich on menus well before 2006. And one of his sources, who worked at a Bronzeville sub shop, claimed it dated back to the 1980s.

"[He] seemed to be an authority on the subject and was happy to share his knowledge of the Jim Shoe," Engler wrote in 2013. "He believed the sandwich originated in the 1980s at a long-closed gyros shop on the far South Side. I can't corroborate the story myself, but it seems that the Jim Shoe does have a long history in the area. In support of this notion, the name is found on an obviously old, professionally painted menu board inside a nearby sub shop."

KARACHI THEORY

Okay, so maybe it did originate in the 1980s at a far South Side sub shop. But that still doesn't tell us who invented it.

Engler speculates that the name of the sandwich may have stemmed from a customer named "Jim" who wanted a customized sandwich, and the guys behind the counter called it "Jim's," and added "shoe" because it sounds more interesting than just "sandwich."

Abdul Wajid, who owned Southtown Sub in Bronzeville, believes the Jim Shoe may have originated in Pakistan. He even goes further to suggest that, based on the preparation of the hot Jim Shoe, it must have been developed by someone from his hometown of Karachi.

This theory comes from the way in which the meat and peppers are chopped and cooked on the griddle in an onomatopoetically named Karachi street food style called "katakat."

"Katakat is famous in my country," Wajid told me as I interviewed him for WBEZ in 2015. "It is one of the top famous dishes from Karachi. You put all the organ parts of the cow and goat—heart, kidney, liver, and brains—and chop and mix them with spice and cook it on a big griddle."

Wajid even had his cook demonstrate by making a "kat-a-kat" sound with his metal spatulas on the griddle. He noted that he even uses traditional Pakistani katakat spice mixtures on the Jim Shoes in his kitchen, "to make it more delicious."

I asked if his background influenced the way he cooked the sandwich.

"My Pakistani background has definitely influenced how I make the Jim Shoe sandwich at Southtown Sub. I can't speak for the other sub shops," he wrote in an interview correspondence translated by his daughter Fariha. "The main feature of the Jim Shoe sandwich is the three different meats, and those aren't common in Pakistani food. The style of chopping is what I used from the Pakistani method of cooking."

So, I asked if all this meant Pakistani cooking had a little influence on the Jim Shoe, too.

"Not little," Wajid said, "almost 90 percent."

At press time, Wajid had left his old Bronzeville location and opened a new Southtown Sub on 71st Street in the Park Manor neighborhood. But Jim Shoes have also traveled well beyond Chicago. By 2020 the sandwich had landed on menus of restaurants from Northern Indiana to Southern Wisconsin. Still, the heart of Jim Shoe-ville will always remain where it took its first steps: Chicago's South Side.

WHERE TO GET A JIM SHOE

Stony Sub
8440 S Stony Island Ave.
773-978-4000

Southtown Sub
112 E. 71st St.
(312) 326-1890

Super Sub & Gyro
2810 W. Marquette Rd.
773-434-2222

18

MALÖRT

David Hammond

MUCH-MALIGNED WORMWOOD-BASED SWEDISH LIQUEUR

Malört bottle. Photo: CH Distillery

At Chicago bars, you can sometimes spot people, usually out-of-towners, eyes squinting, mouths contorted into a mixture of terror and disgust, surrounded by laughing bros. Any local will immediately recognize these to be the telltale symptoms of someone who has taken the plunge by throwing back a first shot of Malört. These tortured expressions are what we call "Malört face."

A kind of amaro, somewhat like Jägermeister or Fernet Branca, Jeppson's Malört is a liqueur that originated in Chicago. For some reason, Malört has a reputation for being almost undrinkable. It's like the old Chicago Cubs before they took the World Series: Malört is rarely thought of as genuinely great, but for whatever reason, Chicagoans have a soft spot in their hearts, and perhaps their heads, for the yellowish spirit.

If you'd purchased a bottle of Malört around the beginning of the twenty-first century, you'd have seen a small marketing card hanging around the neck of the bottle. On that card was the questionable assertion that "During almost 70 years of American distribution, we found only 1 out of 49 men will drink Jeppson's Malört after the first 'shock glass.'" Un-hunh, right. The marketing copy added, in the almost forgotten old-timey language of macho numbskullery, "It takes quite a man to drink Jeppson's Malört."

Clearly, Malört was—and to some extent still is—a drink that's marketed based on its notoriously loathsome taste and its folklore-enshrined ability to function as part of a rite of passage, test of manhood, or both. You'd be hard pressed to find a person who will proclaim that he (much less she) likes the stuff. And yet, Chicagoans and others have great fun with this purportedly undrinkable beverage. Over the years, fans of Malört have created several Malört-related slogans, some of which appear on current packaging:

> Malört, the Champagne of Pain
>
> Malört, tonight's the night you fight your dad
>
> Malört, when you need to unfriend someone IN PERSON

You get the idea: Malört is marketed and, to some extent, "beloved," because its distinctive taste is widely believed to be not particularly good.

CARRYING ON A PROUD TRADITION, OR SOMETHING LIKE THAT

Malört, or Jeppson's Malört Liqueur, is in a line of descent from Beskbrännvin, a colorless Swedish spirit distilled from grain or potatoes. Other similar spirits in the brännvin, or "burnt wine," genre of spirits include brandywine in England and Icelandic brennivín (which, we must admit, pairs very well with the moldy, slightly rotten taste of hakarl, shark that's been buried for a few months and then disinterred to be consumed by Icelanders looking to relive their Viking past).

What sets Malört apart from other "burnt wines" is that it contains wormwood. Malört, in fact, is Swedish for "wormwood." Perhaps it's the first syllable, "mal," that immediately conveys the impression that the beverage is "bad," in line with other mal- constructions like malevolent, malodorous, and so on.

Carl Jeppson came to Chicago from Skåne, Sweden, an area of the Scandinavian country where wormwood grows wild. Wormwood is a bittering agent, most famously included in absinthe, a beverage enjoyed, and made famous by, the late nineteenth–early twentieth century French demimonde and other "bohemians" including Henri de Toulouse-Lautrec, Oscar Wilde, and in the present day, Marilyn Manson (who has his name on a line of absinthe called Mansinth).

It was the wormwood in absinthe, and the chemical thujone in wormwood that was the alleged cause for some of the ill effects—including blindness and madness—attributed to this green spirit. Absinthe was also believed to have psychoactive, hallucinogenic properties. Absinthe with wormwood was banned in the United States and elsewhere after a French workingman, Jean Lanfray, allegedly hammered himself into such an absinthe-induced state of insanity that he murdered his wife and children.

Absinthe with wormwood began to be produced again in the 1990s, when food and beverage laws established by the European Union permitted its renewed manufacture.

Since it started being sold in 1912, Jeppson's Malört has always contained wormwood. Jeppson started selling his creation door to door as a medicinal liquor, which gave him a pass during Prohibition to keep selling the stuff.

Because he put his famous label on the bottles before 1933's Century of Progress, there are only three stars on the flag of Chicago represented above the name of the product, not the four that now appear on the flag; the fourth star was added to the flag in honor of that 1933 celebration, but only the original three stars remain on the Malört label.

Jeppson eventually sold his recipe to Bielzoff Products, a distillery in Chicago. The owner of this distillery, George Brode, bought the distillery from his father-in-law and is credited with marketing Malört beyond the Swedish community. Then Chicago's Polish community took a liking to it. Slowly, Malört became the stuff of legend and hipster bars. Brode hired Pat Gabelick as a secretary in 1966, and when he died in 1999, Gabelick took over the business—even though she is on record for saying she didn't much care for her increasingly popular product. She had one sip years ago, she reported, and that was it.

In the 1970s, though Chicago remained the primary market for Malört, the liqueur was produced for a little while in Kentucky, and then outside Tampa, Florida.

BRINGING MALÖRT TO A NEW GENERATION

On September 28, 2018, the Chicago-based CH Distillery, which had made a name for itself primarily with vodka, bought the Carl Jeppson Company and the Malört brand. As of this writing, CH Distillery produces Malört in its Pilsen distillery.

Tremaine Atkinson, cofounder and distiller at CH Distillery, bought the Malört name and formula from Gabelick, but after some focused tasting sessions that went on for about four months, he and his team realized they had to tweak the original recipe just a little. "Wormwood is the really big flavor in it," Atkinson explained when we got together to chat, "but we had to rebuild the recipe because it tasted out of balance. It also had artificial color in it. We took a look at that and said, 'No, that's not necessary.' So, we figured out how to make it the right color without artificial coloring, and that coloring did change the flavor a little; it's subtle but it's there. The big thing we wanted to get right was the source of the wormwood because not all wormwood is the same; it varies by where it's grown. So, the big challenge was to get the name of the supplier and to gain exclusive access to the Northern European source of the wormwood."

When Atkinson had the chance to purchase the Malört name and associated assets, and move the whole operation to Chicago, he confessed, "I wasn't even that interested in making money on it. I just thought that it would be so cool to do this. Of course, we make a little money on it, but I did it for personal reasons, I liked it, and I thought reputation-wise, it would be good for our business to make Malört."

Though Atkinson believes "90 percent of Malört is consumed in shots," Malört in the early twenty-first century has become an ingredient in cocktails, specifically at "hipster bars." Malört is also paired with Old Style beer for what's called "a Chicago Handshake."

A band called "Malört Face" performs in the area, billing itself as a "Pop Punk/Post-Hardcore s**t show band from Chicago."

Malört is still kind of a funny drink, and Atkinson recognizes that the "gag joke schtick" is part of the reason behind Malört's following. "But it's more than that. It's fun," he says, "and I don't want to lose that. When you hear people's stories about Malört, there's always some joy to it, and it's not going to hurt anybody."

Related to the facial contortions resulting from drinking Malört is the Chicago custom of buying unsuspecting out-of-towners a shot of the spirit and then posting photos of their faces—usually on Instagram—after they down the first (and frequently last) swallow of the stuff. If you're on Instagram, check out the menagerie of winces and grimaces with the hashtag #malortface.

Does Atkinson remember his first shot of Malört? He sure does. "I had just arrived in Chicago and was at a dive bar with a friend. He said, 'You got to try this.' He totally punked me, and I laughed, 'Why the f*** did you do that to me?' It was unexpected, but after a second, I said, 'Hmm. Can I have another one?'"

WHERE TO GET MALÖRT

CH Distillery Tasting Room
564 W. Randolph St.
312-707-8780

Finom Coffee (Malört Chai-Town Latte)
4200 W. Irving Park Rd.
312-620-5010

Binny's Beverage Depot
Multiple locations in and around Chicago

MALÖRT COCKTAIL: THE BITTER END

Ingredients

3 ounces Malört

3 ounces grapefruit juice (preferably freshly squeezed)

Can of radler or shandy (both mix beer and fruit juice, usually lemonade)

Ice

Procedure

1. Fill the glasses halfway with ice cubes.
2. Combine Malört and grapefruit juice in a shaker and shake well.
3. Pour the mixture into your prepped glasses, top with radler or shandy, and serve.

Modified from TheLiquorBarn.com

MAXWELL STREET POLISH

David Hammond

GRIDDLED POLISH SAUSAGE ON A BUN WITH ONIONS, MUSTARD, AND SPORT PEPPERS

Maxwell Street Polish sausage with a sport pepper. Photo: David Hammond

It's two a.m. and it seems half of those in line at Jim's Original plan to sober up by loading a little ballast into the belly before sailing home. The reflection of overhead lights off the yellow walls of this small carry-out stand cast a lustrous golden glow on expectant faces. Everyone seems to be in a good mood, and why not? Many of us here are waiting for a Maxwell Street Polish—a garlicky beef-pork sausage draped with onions, dappled with yellow mustard, studded with sport peppers, hot, greasy, undeniably tasty, and for some, a mouthful of relief for a liquor-lashed tummy.

In the late night–early morning air hangs the sweet-sour scent of steaming onions sitting in brown-white mounds on long griddles running parallel to the front windows. Peek in those windows to see all the main menu items laid out with military precision on the hot metal surface; going from north to south, there are neat formations of sausages, onions, then even more sausages, hamburgers, and more onions.

"Our top-selling item is definitely the Polish sausage," says Jim Christopoulos, grandson of James "Jimmy" Stefanovic, founder and namesake of Jim's Original, when we catch up with him for an interview.

Through sliding windows, people pass their crumpled bills and receive their bulging brown bags, each splashed with a Rorschach of grease. Orders in hand, some customers go to one side of the building where a narrow white counter affixed to the cinder-block wall accommodates those who are cool with eating while standing up. Most customers, however, grab their grub and head to the curb, to their cars, where they eat al trunko, using their hoods or trunks as tabletops or munching their meals as they sit on the bumper and watch the cars stream along the Dan Ryan Expressway.

Jim's Maxwell Street Polish is tastier than a hot dog, with more dimensions of flavor provided by the mix of beef and pork. "The Polish sausage has some garlic in it, and you can see the pepper," says Christopoulos. "We do have an all-beef Polish sausage, but it tastes more like a hot dog."

BORN ON MAXWELL STREET

Jim's has been serving the Maxwell Street Polish since around 1939, when Stefanovic, a Macedonian immigrant, took over his aunt and uncle's stand at the corner of Maxwell and Halsted, dead center of the historic Maxwell Street Market.

Stefanovich had claimed to be the inventor of the sandwich, and it's generally accepted that he was, indeed, the man responsible for popularizing it. If you'd seen his stand in the old days, before it relocated, you'd notice that Polish sausage was the first item listed on Jim's trademark red and yellow signage.

Then as now, the Maxwell Street Polish was a popular item, and there are several factors that might explain the rise of this early fast food.

"Hog butcher for the world," as Carl Sandberg once wrote, Chicago and its Union Stockyards, which closed in 1971, were the source for much of the country's butchered and processed pork and beef. Meat scraps from the stockyards could be used for sausage, and Polish sausage was popular in Chicago for many decades among Polish and other segments of the population (we had it at home all the time). Chicago had always welcomed Eastern European immigrants, due in part to the labor needed in the stockyards (then, as now, meat processing was work for newly arrived immigrants).

"The Halsted Street bus stop was right in front, so we had lots of traffic," says Christopoulos. "The Polish sausage was convenient, cheap, quick, filling, and delicious. It's a one-third pound sausage, so it's a sizeable meal."

"Throughout the 1960s and '70s," says Christopoulos, "the University of Illinois had been saying they're going to close the Maxwell Street Market. We decided to stay there until it was over. The University of Illinois shut us down. Claiming eminent domain, they took the property. My father negotiated to get the location we have. First, we moved to the southwest corner of what used to be Union and O'Brien. In September of 2005, we moved to where we are now."

JIM'S ORIGINAL VS. MAXWELL STREET EXPRESS GRILL

Today, displayed above the carryout windows of Jim's, there's a large sign announcing, "We are not affiliated in any way with any other hot dog stand in the area." Indeed, right next door to Jim's is the competing Express Grill, also open around the clock. Jim's and Express Grill have virtually identical menus.

Predictably, the Express Grill has a sign proclaiming itself as the spot for the Original Maxwell Street Polish. Both Jim's and the Express Grill were located near one another at the old Maxwell Street Market, and they were started by members of the same family. Predictably, there's some intra-family animosity. "My grandfather brought out his sister's son, my mom's cousin, in the late 1960s," Christopoulos says. "My grandfather bought him his first pair of pants, gave him his first job. At some point, he stopped working for my grandfather, and there are family stories about the breakup of that relationship. My understanding is that he opened a store in the Maxwell Street area; it wasn't a success and he closed it. He opened three stores and closed three stores. He opened his fourth store two stores north of us on Halsted. There was a liquor store next to us and then Express Grill. That was in the '80s."

An enduring point of contention among Chicago foodists is "Who has the best Maxwell Street Polish?" On any given day, street food enthusiasts may give the nod to Jim's or the Express Grill.

All over Chicago, there are other quick-service stands offering the "Maxwell Street Polish." Christopoulos, who received his law degree from Chicago's John Marshall Law School (now a part of the University of Illinois at Chicago), told us "I've had to sue three stores that have called themselves 'Jim's something-or-another.' Once the University of Illinois shut [the old Maxwell Street Market] down, we moved, and other stores with the same name started popping up, using the same colors, red and yellow. We didn't trademark anything until 2004. Now we've trademarked 'Jim's' and 'The Original Maxwell Street Polish Sausage.'"

WHERE TO GET A MAXWELL STREET POLISH

Jim's Original
1250 S. Union Ave.
312-733-7820

Express Grill
1260 S. Union Ave.
312-738-2112

The Original Maxwell Street
3801 W. Harrison St.
773-940-2270

HOW TO PREPARE A MAXWELL STREET POLISH AT HOME

Serves 6

Ingredients

Two large onions, sliced
3 tablespoons corn oil
6 sausages, ideally made in Chicago and labeled "Maxwell Street Style"
6 hot dog buns
Sport peppers
Mustard

Procedure

1. Cook the onions in a frying pan with 2 tablespoons oil on medium heat; when translucent, set aside.
2. Cook the sausage in a frying pan with 1 tablespoon oil, on medium to high heat.
3. When sausage is browned, add onions to pan and let the flavors mingle.
4. Put sausages in buns, top with onions, squirt with mustard, and add sport peppers.

MILD SAUCE

Monica Eng

A LITTLE LIKE KETCHUP, A LITTLE LIKE HOT SAUCE, AND MORE THAN JUST BARBECUE SAUCE

Uncle Remus mild sauce on chicken and fries. Photo: Monica Eng

If you order fried food on the South or West Sides, you're going to be asked an important question: "Do you want mild sauce with that?"

A sweet and tart, sometimes spicy elixir, mild sauce adds a distinctive note to fried chicken, french fries, Pizza Puffs (chapter 23), chicken fingers, and all manner of Chicago fast foods. But it also creates distinct confusion for outsiders who give themselves away by answering: "Sorry, do I want what?"

By the end of this chapter, you won't have to make that mistake. You'll learn about the flavor of mild sauce, the camps of mild sauce, the allure of mild sauce, and the story of the man who developed one of the most enduring and consistent mild sauces in Chicago.

MILD SAUCE, DESCRIBED

Most people know mild sauce when they taste it, but the exact formula is very much up for debate. That's largely because, for decades, this orange-to-red condiment was not sold in stores or even restaurant warehouses. Instead, it was most often concocted behind closed doors in independent restaurant kitchens where cooks could give it the heat, sweetness, smoke, or funk unique to that chain or even to a particular location.

Still, it's safe to say that most mild sauces combine elements of ketchup, Kansas or Memphis style barbecue sauce, and Louisiana hot sauce in one reddish, not-too-thick, not-too-thin potion. Ideally, the sauce should cut some of the richness of the fried food with a little acid, while also bathing it in a warm sticky sweetness.

WHERE CAN YOU FIND MILD SAUCE?

You can find mild sauce in most of Chicago's independent South and West Side fast-food restaurants. Most are bare bones, with bulletproof glass at the counter, and offer takeout only. The focus of their menus may differ—with some highlighting beef sandwiches, sub sandwiches, gyros (chapter 14), chicken, or fish—though they all have one thing in common: mild sauce.

Some of the most famous mild sauces come from Chicago chicken restaurants Uncle Remus Saucy Fried Chicken and Harold's Chicken Shack. You'll find the "Harold's" name on dozens of eateries across the city, state, and even in other states. But not all are owned or run by the same people. So, don't expect the mild sauce (or even the chicken) to taste the same at each location.

Uncle Remus, however, offers a popular and more consistent mild sauce. Its three locations are owned and operated by Charmaine Rickette, who took over the business when her parents Gus and Mary Rickette retired in 1999. Anchored by the original West Side location on Madison Street, the business expanded in 2004 to West Suburban Broadview and later opened a South Side location in Bronzeville in 2017.

HOW DO PEOPLE EAT IT?

There are two main ways to eat mild sauce: slathered all over your food before it's packed in the bag or as a side dipper.

You should know which path you plan to take before sidling up to the counter, so you can confidently say "mild on the side, please" or "mild sauce on the chicken, please."

Getting it on the side will usually score you one or two little plastic cups of the stuff. But if you really like the sauce, it's worth splurging for a few extra containers.

Still, Rickette insists the proper way to eat Uncle Remus chicken is to get the sauce applied to the bird before you leave, "so it can marinate," she says. "When I walk in somewhere with a bag of our [saucy] chicken people say, 'Oh my God, I smell Uncle Remus.' You can always tell our chicken by that smell."

I tend to agree with Rickette about getting your chicken already sauced before you take it out, but pre-sauced fries are another story. They can easily turn into mild sauce sponges before you get home, depending on how long your journey takes.

And a word of warning: do not—I repeat, do not—try to eat your hot saucy chicken and fries from the bag while you are driving home. The aromas may be tempting, but saucy fried foods plus driving equal a messy and dangerous ride. Take it from someone who knows. Put the bag in the back seat.

MILD SAUCE CHILDHOOD

If you need more evidence of Chicago's deep cultural segregation, consider this: As a North Sider, I'd never even heard of mild sauce until I was a food-writing adult. But my WBEZ colleague and *The South Side* author Natalie Moore can't remember a time without it.

"I grew up eating it on the South Side, not just on Harold's fried chicken but on Pizza Puffs at Gramps by Morgan Park High School," she said. "You find mild sauce at every kind of hole-in-the-wall takeout joint on the South Side. It's just always there."

And lest you think mild sauce is just doctored ketchup, Moore insists, "It tastes very different from ketchup to me. In fact, I always thought of ketchup as . . . yuck!"

But Moore acknowledges that not all mild sauce is created equal. People have their favorites—and not-so-favorites—even within the same chain. Certain Harold's locations, for instance, are known for their delicious renditions of mild sauce.

"But there are some other Harold's where the mild sauce tastes like straight barbecue sauce," Moore said. "And when you order Lem's [Bar-B-Q] they say, 'Do you want mild sauce?' and I don't know why because it is so clearly barbecue sauce, too."

It's not unusual for folks to have heated discussions about who has the best mild sauce in town. But one thing Moore says she has not heard is a definitive origin story on the sauce. So, she was a little surprised when I told her I thought I found an originator on the West Side.

"I am not saying they are not telling the truth," Moore says. "But in the lore of mild sauce, that origin story has never come up. The lore usually says that we just don't know."

A WEST SIDE MILD SAUCE STORY

So, could it be that South Sider Moore has never heard a mild sauce origin story because the first proprietary mild sauce emerged out of the West Side (the home of Chicago's other big African American population)? Charmaine Rickette at Uncle Remus Saucy Fried Chicken thinks that might be the case.

Now, mind you, she doesn't claim that her family's chicken shops were the first to offer the condiment. Instead, she believes the concept for the first mild sauce emerged when indecisive fried chicken customers were asked a certain question while picking up their food: "Do you want ketchup or hot sauce with that?"

Presumably, they responded with something like: "Hmm, do you have something in between, like a mild sauce?"

And, voilà, the impetus for the first mild sauce was born. Sounds plausible to me. And Rickette said that's exactly how their mild sauce started.

"We did start off in the 1960s by just mixing hot sauce and ketchup like everyone else," Rickette said. "But my dad still was not satisfied with that. So, by the early '70s he started taking official barbecue sauces and working with someone to formulate a sauce by saying 'take this out and take that out,' and we made it our own in that way."

For years, she said, the process required them to take that reformulated barbecue sauce and then add their own "something" to it at the shop. But Rickette said she finally decided to streamline the process.

"More than twenty years ago, I took it to a manufacturer and said, let's put these things together. So here is A and here is B, put them together to make the Uncle Remus mild sauce," she said. "So that's why I said it was proprietary because it is a formula no one else can get. It is not even manufactured in Illinois. That is how much I wanted to protect it."

While some people insist that many mild sauces taste just like barbecue sauces, Rickette says the two sauces play vastly different roles.

"Barbecue sauce will overpower food, while mild sauce balances it out," she says.

To continue finding new uses for it, Rickette keeps a bottle of it in her purse and takes it everywhere she goes.

"I have tested it on all the foods," she says. "Our sauce is good on hot dogs, barbecue, fried chicken, Pizza Puffs (chapter 23), chicken tenders, fish, and Polish sausage. Surprisingly enough, it doesn't taste as good on anyone else's chicken. No offense to Popeye's, but it just doesn't taste the same."

Many note that Rickette's Uncle Remus mild sauce tastes sweeter than South Side mild sauces. Culinary historian Bruce Kraig suggested this might stem from the rural Mississippi roots of West Siders, versus the urban Atlanta and Birmingham roots of South Siders and the accompanying difference in barbecue styles.

When Rickette made the bold move of opening a location of her classic West Side chicken shop on the South Side a few years ago, she figured it would take a while before it gained full acceptance in the community. And how did she gauge that acceptance? With the mild sauce orders, of course.

"When I opened the location on the South Side, most people had never tasted my mild sauce, so 60 to 70 percent were ordering it on the side, like they just wanted to check it out," she recalled of her sweet sauce. "But now that's reversed and nearly 98 percent of my customers get it on the chicken."

So even if hers wasn't the first mild sauce in the city—and, by the way, no one else is making that claim—it is one of the most consistent, enduring, and well loved.

"People are in love with our sauce," says Rickette. "It is so endearing, the things they say about it. They say it's like crack, and I don't take that as an offense. I take it as, well, that's the way they describe it. It's definitely a Chicago thing."

Today, Rickette sells her sauce at her three Uncle Remus locations, but also online at www.UncleRemusUsa.com. You can also find Harold's Chicken mild sauce on sale at https://www.haroldschickendowntown.com/.

GUS RICKETTE'S STORY

Gus Rickette, Charmaine's father, may be the inventor of mild sauce—or just the last man standing who made his own proprietary formula—but even more impressive than his story of creating a mild sauce is his story of creating a business.

He talked to my Chewing Podcast cohost Louisa Chu for a 2017 show and told her about his arrival in Chicago and the way it shaped his view of the world. At the time of the interview, he was ninety-one years old.

"It was such a story that sometimes you don't want it to be told," he began. "I migrated here from [Leland,] Mississippi, 1943. I just had a mother and didn't know my father. I was an only child, and I was very lonely.

"When I came to Chicago, I didn't know anyone and I didn't have any money," said Rickette, who was born in 1926. "I think I had about ten cents in my pocket at that time . . . I was walking and trying to find my way to the West Side of Chicago, where I thought I knew some people, and I was picked up by the police. I was put in jail because I had a little knife that I was using to eat an apple. And, well, that sounds bad, but it turned out to be a blessing because I didn't have no place to stay anyway. I had been sleeping on the streets and in doorways with the rest of the bums."

Rickette was part of the second wave of the Great Migration to Chicago. During that wave, the African American population in the city almost tripled, leaving housing scarce.

"I found a job [washing dishes] but I still didn't have a bed because the West Side, it was so small and there were more Blacks migrating than you had accommodations for," he recalled. "There was no place for me, so I would go back downtown every night and I learned to sneak into the theaters. When the ticket girl would go to sleep, I would sneak in and sleep in a chair. The next morning, I would get up and go to work. I had a job, but I had no bed. That was my life.

"That's the foundation that made me," he said. "It destroyed some people, but it heightened my determination."

Eventually Rickette found work as a janitor and in the brickyards, and he sent for his wife Mary, who came up from Mississippi and worked in Chicago factories. By the early 1960s, he said, a business opportunity came along.

"I had a friend from back home, and we grew up together," Rickette remembered. "He was in a little better financial condition than I was. He was doing some illegal things at that time, and he gave me money, his money to keep. It was his vision that we should go in business together. So, I bought a business with him in 1963 on Pulaski and Madison."

The business was called G & G Chicken Shack, "but very soon my friend passed away, and I became the complete owner of the business."

According to the Uncle Remus website, the original restaurant had one refrigerator, one fryer, and one box of chicken. A half of a fried chicken sold for one dollar. Rickette later changed the name of the restaurant to the Royal Chicken Shack and researched ways to create a perfect piece of chicken.

"I was carried away about fried chicken, studying the fried chicken I'd been eating, and I developed a better system to be better and faster," he said. "We were too slow [when frying everything to order] so I learned to use warmers and that was successful."

During the 1968 riots in the wake of the assassination of Dr. Martin Luther King, Rickette says, his chicken shack had been damaged, and he needed a new sign. Instead, he got a new name.

"We went to the sign store where a [white] individual out of Indiana had ordered a sign [for Uncle Remus fried chicken]," he said. "But because of the riots between Black people and whites, the individual changed his mind and didn't want the sign no more. So, the owner told me I could have it at a good price, and I bought that sign."

In 1969, with a brand-new sign, he rebranded his business Uncle Remus.

In the ensuing years, Rickette opened and closed several shops, but always held onto his flagship Madison Street location on the West Side. Still, he said, he never forgot where he came from or his time as a homeless Chicagoan.

"Sometimes I still weep today," he said wiping away his tears. "I'm sorry, but when you don't have a place to stay, it, well . . . yeah, we should always help the poor."

Charmaine Rickette said these early experiences left her father with a soft spot in his heart for people who need a helping hand.

"We try to employ returning citizens as much as we can," she says. "It's almost a joke here that to get a job [at Uncle Remus] you have to be an ex- something . . . But that is where he came from, and he always had a passion to make sure that these people were welcomed here and could have a job."

WHERE TO GET MILD SAUCE

Uncle Remus Saucy Fried Chicken
5611 W. Madison St.
773-261-7311

Harold's Fried Chicken
(locations throughout Chicagoland)

Pretty much any South or West side fast-food restaurant.

You can also now find Uncle Remus and Harold's mild sauce sold online.

21

MOTHER-IN-LAW

David Hammond

CHICAGO CORN ROLL TAMALE WITH CHILI AND TRADITIONAL CHICAGO HOT DOG CONDIMENTS

Fat Johnnie's shack. Photo: David Hammond

Since 1972, Fat Johnnie's Famous Red Hots in Marquette Park on Chicago's South Side has been housed in what is lovingly referred to as "the shack." This tumble-down wooden building, with hand-painted signage and menu, looks as though it was hit by a hurricane; there are few right angles on the grubby, wobbly-looking white building, which has a sloping wooden awning in front. It does not look like the most promising place to grab lunch. It is, however, a landmark of Chicago food greatness, being what some believe to be the home of the Mother-in-Law: a Chicago corn roll tamale (chapter 6) in a hot dog bun, covered in chili, dressed like a dragged-through-the-garden Chicago hot dog (chapter 9).

Fat Johnnie's is owned and operated by John Pawlikowski, who lives next door to "the shack." Pawlikowski started the business by selling hot dogs (advertised on his street-side signage as "Fit for a King"). Pawlikowski explained that "I worked with a Lithuanian man at Nabisco when I was eighteen years old, and he showed me how to make them with a pushcart, and the concept of this hot dog stand is built on the concept of a pushcart. There's no french fries, just hot dogs and Polish sausage."

When Anthony Bourdain came to Chicago for an episode of *No Reservations*, one of his stops was at Fat Johnnie's, where he chomped into a Mother-in-Law after pronouncing it "the evil stepbrother of the hot dog."

John T. Edge, James Beard Award winner and director of the Southern Foodways Alliance, visited Fat Johnnie's, ate a Mother-in-Law, and declared that he loved it.

Bourdain's and Edge's assessments of the Mother-in-Law are not mutually exclusive. It is an odd culinary creation that makes some people uncomfortable but that still has a devoted following. Bourdain called the Mother-in-Law "perhaps the greatest, most uniquely Chicago food invention."

The Mother-in-Law sandwich consists of a Chicago corn roll tamale, nestled into a bun, covered in chili, and dressed with some or all the traditional Chicago hot dog accoutrements: weird blue-green relish, mustard, onions, pickle, and sport peppers. Sometimes cheese is added, and at that point, the sandwich technically becomes what Fat Johnnie's refers to as a Father-in-Law. It's a delicious mess, so good that you will probably eat through the whole thing before realizing that you're wearing a good portion of it on your chest.

Incidentally, about the name. The Mother-in-Law was allegedly so named because it, too, will give you heartburn (apologies to all mothers-in-law, everywhere).

MEXICAN AMERICAN FOOD?

Standing outside the Witches' Market in Mexico City, close to the ruined Aztec pyramids of Tenochtitlán, we were attracted to the vendor with the longest line—must be the good stuff, right? The vendor served a standard Mexican breakfast food, a guajolota, a tamale in a Mexican roll called a bolillo, drenched with salsa verde. A traditional Mexican green sauce is called salsa de suegra, "Mother-in-Law" sauce. Perhaps the Mother-in-Law as served at Fat Johnnie's is a stateside version of a south-of-the-border sandwich.

According to the Southern Foodways Alliance, the tamale was brought to the United States by Mexican workers who may have packed a few tamales for lunch when they went to work in the fields. In those fields, specifically in the Mississippi Delta, Mexicans would have encountered African Americans and shared their tamales.

During the Great Migration from the Delta to Chicago, African Americans brought the tamales with them. Later, in the style of the guajolota, tamales were served in the sandwich called the Mother-in-Law, though instead of green salsa de suegra, red chili sauce doused the tamales.

A MOTHER-IN-LAW, HOLD THE BUN

The tamale boat or chili tamale is a variation on the Mother-in-Law: a Chicago-style corn roll tamale in a bowl of chili, dressed with chopped onions, sport peppers, and perhaps oyster crackers. If cheese is added, you have a chili cheese tamale.

I'd enjoyed an outstanding version of the chili cheese tamale at Parky's Hot Dogs in Forest Park outside Chicago. It was so good, in fact, that I went back the next day with my brother. We ordered our chili cheese tamales and sat down to eat, and eat we did, enthusiastically. Less than a minute later, an older guy who was picking up his lunch at the counter tripped over the rubber carpeting and fell into the plate glass window, shattering it. We went over to help him up. There was a little blood, but he looked just a little shaken; he said he was okay, and paramedics arrived almost immediately, and so we sat back down to finish our chili cheese tamales, appetites undiminished. The chili cheese tamales were that good.

Fat Johnnie's has been going strong for over forty years, and the place, though some might consider it a touch shabby, is beloved as an old shoe and just as comfortable. Though Johnnie tells us that he gets a lot of tourists, it's likely the local neighborhood is the primary customer base (as it is for most successful restaurants). Here's an example of that neighborly love. When Fat Johnnie's cashier, Corinne Kopsky, had some medical issues, they put out a donation jar by the window and customers kicked in about five thousand dollars. At a hot dog stand!

TALE OF TWO JOHNNIES

Over the years, others have served the Mother-in-Law, most notably Johnny O's (3465 South Morgan), which closed in September of 2019. As is so often the case, there is contention about which Johnnie invented this quirky sandwich.

"I don't even know how the Mother-in-Law got its name, but I used to sell it off a pushcart when I was a kid, 11 or 12 years old," Johnny Veliotis told DNAinfo in 2015. "We used to put a hot tamale on a bun and what made ours special was that we threw the kitchen sink on it. So, years ago, for 5 cents you got a meal."

A WORD ABOUT FAT JOHNNIE'S MIGHTY DOG

Pushing the limits, Fat Johnnie's also offers the Mighty Dog, which has both the Chicago corn roll tamale and a Chicago hot dog in the bun, along with the chili and condiments. Having the juicy wiener in there significantly moistens each bite and helps this carb-heavy sandwich "go down" more easily.

WHERE TO GET A MOTHER-IN-LAW OR TAMALE BOAT/CHILI TAMALE/CHILI CHEESE TAMALE

Fat Johnnie's Famous Red Hots
7242 S. Western Ave.
773-633-8196

Parky's Hot Dogs
329 Harlem Ave.
708-366-3090

Micky's Gyros
10701 S. Roberts Road
Palos Hills, IL
708-974-0880

22

PEPPER AND EGG SANDWICH

David Hammond

SWEET PEPPERS AND SCRAMBLED EGGS ON BREAD

Pepper and egg sandwich. Photo: Buona Beef

The pepper and egg sandwich is a meal that could hardly be simpler to prepare, and the name says it all: peppers (sweet bell peppers, usually green, though sometimes red or yellow) and eggs (usually scrambled) on bread (a roll or a segment of French bread), which in our experience is usually served room temperature, neither warmed nor chilled. Individual vendors sometimes add onions, Parmesan, and spices like oregano to make their sandwiches slightly different from what's being offered by the competition (and in Chicago, there are lots of places offering pepper and egg sandwiches).

Though it has been claimed that the sandwich was created by immigrants who came to Chicago from Italy in the late nineteenth century and early twentieth century, it would be exceedingly difficult to support the claim that Chicago is the first place where the pepper and egg sandwich was made.

The sandwich is so basic, using ingredients that would be found in many kitchens, that it seems highly likely that a home cook started preparing pepper and egg sandwich before these popular non-meat meals became common on menus. There's no denying, however, that pepper and egg sandwiches are quite popular in Chicago.

HOW THE SANDWICH BECAME A HIT IN CHICAGO

The popularity of the meatless pepper and egg sandwich is likely due to the large Catholic population in the city—and, ironically, to the popularity of the Italian beef sandwich (chapter 15) and the many Italian beef stands in the city.

Chicago has always had a large Catholic population; as of 2021, 36 percent of Chicagoans identified as Catholic. Part of the reason for this may be that Chicago has always welcomed immigrants, many coming from Catholic countries, including Poland, Italy, and, most recently, Mexico.

The Catholic church has traditionally guided followers to fast on Fridays. Since 1965, the Church limited fasting to just those Fridays during Lent, the six-week span from Ash Wednesday to Easter. On those fasting days, Catholics seek out foods other than meat, including fish, eggs, and vegetables.

The Italian beef stand got its start in the city's Italian neighborhoods. Even though the sandwich was not part of the culinary folkways these Italian Americans might have known in the Old Country, once in Chicago they embraced this sandwich as their own.

Owners of the traditional Italian Beef stand didn't want to lose business on fasting days, so someone had the bright idea to use the rolls or bread, usually French bread segments, already used for the beef sandwiches, as well as the sweet peppers, also used on the beef sandwiches, to make a meal suitable for those who were abstaining from meat or who simply wanted something a little different.

Many Italian beef stands had a grill for heating up hamburgers and the like, and the hot metal surface could as easily be deployed for cooking scrambled eggs.

The pepper and egg sandwich is a fine meal, and it was enjoyed for breakfast long before quick service restaurants started serving egg muffins and breakfast burritos.

Though the Catholic Church has relaxed the rules regarding the need to fast without meat on Fridays, Buona Beef, with many locations all over the Chicago area, serves a darn good pepper and egg sandwich (with added Parmesan), but only on Fridays.

Perhaps it's testament to the general popularity of the pepper and egg sandwich that White Palace Grille, the now-closed Fiore's Delicatessen, and others like it, offer the sandwich, as the Fiore's counterman once told us, "Every day, all year long."

Pro tip: this is a wholesome, though not hugely flavorful, sandwich. To bring it up a notch, add some giardiniera, which will be available at most Italian beef stands that offer the pepper and egg sandwich.

WHERE TO GET A PEPPER AND EGG SANDWICH

Bari Subs and Italian Food
1120 W. Grand Ave.
312-666-0730

Buona Beef
(multiple locations)
6801 Roosevelt Rd.
Berwyn, IL
708-749-2555

White Palace Grill
1408 W. Madison St.
312-226-9529

HOW TO PREPARE A PEPPER AND EGG SANDWICH AT HOME

Serves 1

Ingredients

2 eggs
1 sweet pepper
1–2 ounces oil (olive, canola, or vegetable oil)
Roll or French bread segment

Instructions

1. Slice the sweet pepper into strips about an inch wide and pan fry in oil.
2. Remove peppers when they're soft.
3. Scramble eggs as you usually would.
4. Put it all on a bun and done.

23

PIZZA PUFF

Monica Eng

A FRIED DOUGH PILLOW FILLED WITH TOMATO SAUCE, CHEESE, AND OTHER INGREDIENTS

Pizza Puff on a plate. Photo: Monica Eng

The story of this treat is an unlikely one of an Assyrian immigrant who built an empire on Chicago-style tamales, and how his grandson expanded that empire by making fried pizzas out of tortillas.

Like a lot of Chicago's famous treats, the Pizza Puff is a snack born of competition, cross-cultural innovation and a lot of trial and error. Specifically, it was spurred by the mid-century proliferation of pizzerias and a need for hot dog stands to hold their own against them.

So, hold on to your french fries, this is going to be a fun ride.

WHAT IS A PIZZA PUFF?

Although the Pizza Puff is sold in thirty-eight states, about half of all puffs are eaten in the Chicago area. So, for all you uninitiated out-of-towners, think of a crispy fried pillow stuffed with hot Italian meat sauce and melty cheese—one that satisfies your craving for dairy, meat, and fried carbs all in a single bite.

While researching this chapter, I heard a lot of Pizza Puff stories from enthusiasts. Some told me about stress-eating them while working long hours on a political campaign. Others reminisced about snacking on them with mild sauce in high school. But many recalled them as the perfect snack to grab after a long night of revelry.

Still, none prepared me for the flaky, pastry-like, savory hand pie that I discovered when I finally tasted one. (Yes, shame on me for waiting half a century.) These days I've enjoyed them more than once, eaten with knife and fork next to a salad and a nice glass of red wine.

WHERE DID IT COME FROM?

To understand the Pizza Puff, first you need to understand Chicago corn roll tamales (chapter 6). These Chicago-style tamales are tasty little tubes of cornmeal and chili-like meat traditionally wrapped in parchment paper and sold at hot dog stands—sometimes standing in for a Chicago hot dog (chapter 9).

While Supreme and Tom Tom lead the tamale manufacturing pack, another veteran in this field is the Illinois Tamale Company (Iltaco), started by Elisha Shabaz in the 1920s. Iltaco still makes tamales today, but in the last half-century the company became even more famous for, you guessed it, the Pizza Puff.

FROM TAMALES TO PIZZA PUFFS

An Assyrian immigrant who fled Iran around the turn of the twentieth century, Elisha Shabaz came to Chicago and started a business selling condiments and "hot dog carts made out of old baby buggies with Sternos," according to his great grandson Adam Shabaz, who runs Iltaco today.

One of his customers, Adam says, was an Armenian immigrant who fell ill and couldn't pay his bill. When he eventually died, his widow said she had no money to pay off their debt. "She said, 'All I have is our tamale recipe,' and she gave it to our great grandfather," Adam Shabaz says.

In 1927, Elisha used that recipe to establish the Illinois Tamale Company, which could now also supply tamales to his clients' pushcarts.

Fast-forward to the early 1970s. At this point, hot dog pushcarts had been almost entirely replaced by hot dog stands with bigger menus and deep fryers. Elisha's grandson Warren was running the Iltaco business and starting to hear concerns about another popular fast food.

"While delivering the tamales to a lot of these hot dog stands, our father saw pizzerias popping up everywhere," Shabaz said. "And he started getting more and more questions [from hot dog stand clients] about some sort of pizza product because . . . they needed to compete in some way."

Like so many other Chicago fast-food innovations, this one needed to be delicious and work seamlessly with equipment that was already in the restaurant's kitchen. So, Warren Shabaz zeroed in on creating something that could be cooked in the hot dog stand's deep fryer.

"He kind of looked at the idea of a burrito—something with filling fully enclosed in a tortilla," Adam said. "And he started messing with that."

Warren's other son, Andrew Shabaz (who is the Executive VP of Sales & Marketing at Iltaco), said his father knew they wanted to make something like the calzones they saw in their Italian neighborhood, but it required a lot of trial and error.

"I think the epiphany was finally finding how to create this item that could be cooked in the fryer every time without actually exploding," Andrew Shabaz said.

"Yeah," his brother Adam concurred. "If you mess up the oil in their fryer you are never going to have that customer again. They will hate you because they are using that oil for fish, chicken, fries, and everything else."

By 1976 Warren Shabaz had finally perfected his creation—a frozen packet filled with pork, tomato sauce, and cheese that wouldn't explode in the deep fryer. Early packaging featured a picture of a mustachioed Pizza Puff character exclaiming, "Atsa Gooood!"

YES, IT'S A TORTILLA

The big difference between a traditional Italian calzone or panzerotti and the Pizza Puff is essentially one thing: the wrapper. The two Italian snacks use raw dough for the crust while Warren Shabaz pragmatically opted for a much easier option: Mexican flour tortillas.

Despite the multi-cultural mixing, tortillas made sense since they were so widely available in Chicago. But at a certain point, Adam said, their tortilla supplier cried "Uncle!"

"He said, 'We appreciate the business, but we just can't keep up,' and he suggested we go out and get our own tortilla press," Adam recalled. "I think our first one could press out four dough balls at a time."

Today, the company has gotten a lot faster in its tortilla making and still proudly lists "flour tortilla" right on the front of the package.

IN YOUR FROZEN FOOD AISLE

Over the decades the Pizza Puff has expanded into thirty-eight states, added several new flavors, and even landed a spot in the frozen food aisle.

In 1978, Iltaco launched an all-beef puff, which has become the dominant variety in Chicago fast-food shops. In 1980, the ham and cheese puff joined the lineup, featuring a female Pizza Puff character who exclaims, "Cool Dude!"

Eventually, Iltaco would introduce more than a dozen different "puff" flavors including buffalo chicken, pepperoni pizza, taco puffs, gyros puffs, and the most recent Reuben puff.

Over the years, the company has aggressively guarded its name and logo, successfully winning a 2018 suit against a competitor who attempted to use both.

Despite their expansion, Adam says they try to grow in a measured way, as needed.

"We're always doing things out of need until it gets too cumbersome, and then we make the investment to grow on a larger scale," he said. "So, we make all our dough from scratch, and we press it out every day and make our fillings from scratch. We grind fresh pork and beef every single day. We try to get it as close to a natural a product as possible, to make something we ourselves enjoy."

Despite the original intent to make a snack that would give pizzerias a run for their money, the Shabazes' Pizza Puffs haven't exactly closed down the Italian pizza market. Instead, they've done something much more special. They've taken their own place in the canon of Chicago "hot dog stand" fare that, like Chicago corn roll tamales, tell unlikely stories of the city's fascinating immigrant and cultural history.

Note: During this research, I found references to something called a Pizza Puff produced by Arco Frozen Foods out of Allendale, New Jersey, but no current records of that company exist.

WHERE TO GET PIZZA PUFFS

You can find Pizza Puffs in many Chicago fast-food stands and even online.

24

RAINBOW CONE

Monica Eng

A CAKE CONE PILED HIGH WITH FIVE SUPER-SPECIFIC FLAVORS STACKED IN A VERY PARTICULAR ORDER TO FORM A SMALL RAINBOW

Katherine Sapp stands next to the original Rainbow Cone, which opened as a small stand on 92nd Street in 1926. A few years later, it moved across the street into larger digs.
Photo Courtesy of Rainbow Cone.

In the mid-1920s, the corner of 92nd and Western Avenue was a remote outpost in a rural part of Chicago called Beverly. But where some people saw emptiness, Joe Sapp saw opportunity.

Banking on the flow of weekend visitors to huge nearby cemeteries, as well as an anticipated Western Avenue streetcar, he opened a little hut called the Rainbow Lodge in 1926.

"Western Avenue was a dirt road, but he knew the streetcar was coming and it was going to grow," said his granddaughter, Lynn Sapp. "Down on 111th Street there was [Mount Greenwood] cemetery, and so he knew that the traffic would be coming back his way every Sunday when people made the trip there."

Mourners were well known for stopping at bars on their way back from the cemetery, but Sapp knew that some families would need other kinds of places to gather as well—especially during prohibition.

"So, he thought that maybe they would bring sandwiches, but also [bring] enough money for a cone," Sapp said.

Still, this couldn't be just any old cone. Instead, Sapp said, her grandpa wanted to make something unique, bright, and theatrical, something that was worth the splurge of twelve cents.

"Back then you could get a whole blue plate special—like a whole plate of food—for a dime, so twelve cents for a cone was a lot of money," Sapp said.

In the end, he thought up a treat that would deliver "something unique and full of fruits and nuts for that money."

That something unique turned out to be Sapp's signature Rainbow Cone—a multi-layer cone featuring at least three kinds of nuts and three kinds of fruits in a concoction that still attracts customers to the corner of 92nd and Western a century later.

WHAT IS A RAINBOW CONE?

According to Lynn Sapp, this iconic cone has changed very little since 1926. For most of the Rainbow Cone history, she says, the treat has featured a pointy cake cone piled high with five super-specific flavors stacked in a very particular order to form a small rainbow.

From bottom to top, these flavors are chocolate, strawberry, Palmer House (featuring cherry-walnut vanilla), pistachio, and orange sherbet.

While this may not sound like the most logical combination of flavors on paper, Sapp says her grandfather thought long and hard about how each taste would interact with the others—and you can't argue with success.

"The combination really works, and the flavors blend together so well whether you are licking from the top to the bottom or the bottom to the top," she says.

"He also wanted to make sure he was giving something with a lot of substance, which is why he put so many fruits and nuts in it. It had real strawberries back in the day, then the cherries and walnuts [in the Palmer House], as well as orange and almonds and pistachios when they could get then. He wanted it to

The original Rainbow Cone features five idiosyncratic flavors. Photo: Monica Eng.

have substance and calories—because, back then, they weren't worried about calories; in fact, they wanted them."

Sapp says this exact combination—with one substitution—has been at the heart of the Rainbow Cone for almost a century.

"[At one time] we also had maple-nut on the cone—which I guess was a big deal back in the day—but the profile didn't fit with the Rainbow Cone," she said. "So, they dropped that one, and they put in the Palmer House instead."

WAIT, PALMER HOUSE? WHAT'S THAT FLAVOR ALL ABOUT?

For many people, the Palmer House layer of ice cream is the real star of the Rainbow Cone. But its exact origins are unclear. Most Chicagoans might assume the flavor was connected to the famous downtown Chicago Palmer House hotel that opened in 1875.

But Sapp says the flavor arrived with her grandfather when he showed up in Chicago from New York via Ohio, "and it had nothing to do with the Chicago hotel."

I have not been able to find any historical references in newspaper archives that connect cherry-walnut ice cream to the famous Palmer House. Instead, it's only mentioned in conjunction with the Rainbow Cone. But wherever the flavor came from, it's a smooth, vanilla delight packed with lots of fresh walnuts and sweet cherries.

THE STACKING STRATEGY

Joe Sapp was an orphan, a tool maker, and huge ice cream fan. Those tool-making skills would end up playing a key role in his success as an ice cream man. See, stacking five flavors with a regular scoop would produce a perilously tippy tower of treats and potentially bad experience for all involved. So, Sapp devised another way.

"He built his own ice cream spade, which was specifically designed to scrape and stack the ice cream," Lynn Sapp said. "He was a really creative guy who was a machinist and created his own tools. The spade was the perfect tool to scrape and stack the ice cream from our brine-cooled ice cream boxes, which we still had when I bought the store in 1986."

But while Joe was the creative force behind the operation, Lynn says it was her grandmother, Katharine, who was the financial brain behind the Rainbow Cone.

"She was a good businesswoman who didn't tolerate waste," Sapp said. "She kept the business going strong right through the Depression when people didn't have a lot of money for extras. She had the whole family working and employed my aunts and uncles. I mean we always had adults working there. No kids . . . And there were no business loans at that time, so she had to make sure they had the money to pay for the original store and the one they built across the street where we are still working today."

During World War II, Sapp said the shop became a gathering place for news. Her grandfather would sit in the yard with a big radio letting people hear and discuss current events.

During the 1960s and '70s, Sapp's father Robert took over the business with his wife, Jean, and raised their kids in a house behind the store. Sapp bought the business in 1986.

EXPANSION AND CAKE

As Rainbow Cone approaches its hundred-year mark, the brand is staying strong. Sapp says the ice cream is still made by a local dairy and ice cream manufacturer using a proprietary company recipe. In 2016, she opened another Rainbow Cone hut about the same size as the tiny original, but this time on Navy Pier. Sapp has also introduced Rainbow Cone cake rolls.

"When I first bought the business, everyone I knew was getting married, and I had to bring something to the showers, so I started doing my own rainbow cake rolls. I made my own butter cream and everything," she said. "That's how it progressed into the cake roll we have today that is fantastic."

Today folks no longer have to trudge all the way out to 92nd and Western (or even Navy Pier) to get a taste of the famous cone. The chain has partnered with Buona Beef to open suburban satellite locations and even a North Side location.

There are now multiple Rainbow Cone trucks that travel the city (and even one in Florida) posting their locations on social media. Sapp has also partnered with delivery services that will bring a frozen packaged version of the cone to you anywhere in the Chicago area.

A few years ago, after ninety years of winter closings, Sapp decided to keep the shop open all year-round, allowing locals to enjoy this uniquely Chicago rainbow any time of year.

The quirky cone may not be as hard to find as it once was, but it just makes trips out to the weird pink stucco building on Western Avenue all the more special—kind of like a destination outing. You stand in line looking at the vintage Rainbow Cone photos. You commiserate with fellow enthusiasts about the first time you had one. Then you finally get that crazily stacked cone (with a special guard to keep it from dripping), take your first lick, and taste a century of eccentric Chicago history melting in your mouth.

"Wow, it really works," my usually grumpy son told me as he dug in to his first Rainbow Cone. "Definitely worth the trip."

WHERE TO GET THE RAINBOW CONE

The Original Rainbow Cone
9233 S. Western Ave.
773-238-9833

The Original Rainbow Cone
498 E. Roosevelt Rd.
Lombard, IL
630-692-1134

The Original Rainbow Cone
Navy Pier
600 E. Grand Ave.
773-238-9833

The Original Rainbow Cone
3754 W. Touhy Ave.
Skokie, IL

The Original Rainbow Cone
7417 S. Cass Ave.
Darien, IL
630-963-2333

In 2022, Rainbow Cone partnered with Buona Beef, which offers the famous cone at several locations.

RIB TIPS

Monica Eng

THE GNARLY, FATTY, DELICIOUS ENDS CUT OFF A RACK OF SMOKED ST. LOUIS SPARERIBS

Rib tips from Lem's BBQ in Chicago. Photo: Monica Eng

Kansas has its baby backs. Texas has its brisket and links. North Carolina has its pulled pork.

And Chicago has a cut superior to all of them: fatty, gristly, meaty rib tips.

Overlooked by some cooks as junk cuts, rib tips are turned into barbecue gold by South Side cooks using metal pits under tempered glass chambers that look a lot like huge aquariums.

So how did this all start?

Chicago pitmaster, author, and barbecue historian Gary Wiviott says he's not sure who served the first commercial rib tip, but that it followed the longstanding pattern of African Americans finding ways to coax the best out of less valued cuts.

He notes that the tips are produced when butchers trimmed the ends off a rack of St Louis spareribs to make them perfectly symmetrical.

"That rack is meaty and pretty and fits on a plate, and the people on the North Side want that," he says. "So instead of throwing [the trimmed bits] away, what a lot of restaurants used to do is make it a cook's treat out of this gnarly and chewy cut that you didn't want to give the customer."

But by the 1960s, there was at least one restaurateur in Chicago who did decide to serve them to customers.

BIRTH OF RIB TIPS

His name was Myles Lemons. He and his brother Bruce arrived in Chicago from Indianola, Mississippi, in the 1940s. In 1954, Myles and Bruce opened a barbecue house called Lem's, at 59th and State Street, and invited their brother James to join the business with a second location on 75th Street that opened in 1968.

"One day, I think it was in the early to mid-'60s, Myles came up with an idea for using those tips, because for years they would throw that part away," said Carmen Lemons, who runs the business today. "He said, 'Let's cook them and see what comes of it.' And it turned out to be a good thing."

Lemons, whose father was James, says her uncle treated the tips the same way they cooked their signature links and ribs—by smoking them over charcoal and hickory wood in their signature aquarium smoker and slathering them in Uncle Myles's sweet, tangy sauce.

First, she said, her uncle Myles just fed them to the staff. But they were so good that he decided to put them on the menu, hacked into chubby matchbox-sized pieces, perfect for feeding a crowd.

"They are better for families to feed off because they are not as expensive," Lemons said. "Now we sell large and small combos, and people like them because there is just as much meat on them as there is on the ribs—even more."

Indeed, what the tips lack in beauty and continuity they make up for in lusciousness. Some of the barky chunks are streaked with fat, others are bisected by bone, and most are dotted with chewy knobs of cartilage—that you can chomp like a piece of gum between your jaws until they dissolve.

To round out the meal, rib tip orders often come nestled between sauce-soaked fries and a soft white blanket of Wonder Bread. All the better to soak up every drop of the zingy sauce.

Buckets of tips may be perfect to eat with friends and family, but they're less ideal for a first date. This is not just because each piece requires a custom plan of attack that could require awkwardly fishing something out of your mouth, but because their sheer delectability can trigger fits of meat inhalation that might be better left for the second date.

A FADING ART

Today, Chicago still has several South and West Side spots producing notable aquarium smoked rib tips, including Honey One, Uncle Johns, Alice's, and of course Lem's.

Lemons and her sister Lynn Walker took over the nearly seventy-year-old business fully after their father James passed away in 2015. The 59th and State location closed in the 1980s, but at the 75th Street location, Lemons says she tries to keep things as traditional as possible, including using the same brand of aquarium smoker from Avenue Metal "that we have been using since 1954."

But she says it is getting harder and harder to find people to learn to cook on this specialized piece of equipment. Aquarium smoking relies on instinct, experience, and knowledge of when to hose down the fire a bit or move pieces of meat to different levels of the smoker.

"It's an art," she said of the instinctual aquarium process. "You have to be trained to cook on that pit for at least a month, and we are concerned that, as we get older, it gets hard to find people to learn to cook like that."

She said they have a special technique for getting the rib tips just right that involves cooking the meat in the aquarium smoker off the direct heat for hours, "and that makes it really tender," Lemons said, "then you finally bring that down and put it on the pit itself . . . But this takes someone who stands up there working with the charcoal and the hickory wood and knowing when to turn it and sear [the meat]."

THE FUTURE OF AQUARIUM SMOKED RIB TIPS

Wiviott is worried that this unique Chicago style of cooking pork is going to fade away after this generation of South Side barbecue purveyors passes on.

"It's just too hard for people," he said. "Maybe there will be a renaissance—and there have been some new places—but you're never gonna put four kids through private school and buy new cars and pay off your house running a BBQ joint like this. You are just going to work your ass off and probably lose a few fingers while butchering your meat."

For now, Lemons said she and her sister are pleased that they have kept the business going strong, even through the COVID pandemic. They celebrated Lem's sixty-fifth anniversary in 2019 and are even offering franchising opportunities for others.

"We are trying to do the best we can to keep it alive," she says. "We hope that it doesn't die out because people love our rib tips and that charcoal hickory wood flavor."

They also love the intoxicating scent that comes whispering out of Lem's tall smokestack perfuming of the neighborhood with that signature aroma.

"My father James always told us, if there's no smoke, it's not real barbecue."

WHERE TO GET RIB TIPS

Lem's Bar-B-Q
311 E 75th St
773-994-2428

Alice's Bar-B-Que
65 E 43rd St
773-924-3843

Honey 1 BBQ
746 E 43rd St
773-285-9455

26

SHRIMP DEJONGHE

David Hammond

BAKED SHRIMP WITH GARLIC, BUTTER, AND BREADCRUMBS

Shrimp DeJonghe at Hugo's Frog Bar. Photo: Kailley Lindman

Like chicken Vesuvio (chapter 5), shrimp DeJonghe is one of those dishes that might cause you to wonder, "Really? No one—like someone in maybe Greece or Italy—thought of sautéed shrimp with garlic and butter before three Belgian brothers gave us shrimp DeJonghe?"

There's little doubt that someone did probably think of this dish before it showed up on the menu of the DeJonghe Restaurant, but it was there that the dish was so named, and that name has stuck, perhaps in part because it sounds fancy, and the dish is designed to be served in a perhaps more formal dining room setting than, say, a Chicago hot dog (chapter 9) or an Italian beef (chapter 15).

IT HAPPENED AT THE WORLD'S COLUMBIAN EXPOSITION

Like so many other foods, shrimp DeJonghe's popularity can be traced to the World's Columbian Exposition of 1893. This massive fair was to prove a high-visibility venue for the introduction of many innovative foods, including Cracker Jack, Juicy Fruit, and Cream of Wheat.

Brothers Henri, Pierre, and Charles de Jonghe came over from Belgium to serve food at this late-nineteenth century fair, and things went so well that they decided to stay in Chicago and open a restaurant. The brothers opened their first place in the basement of the old Masonic Temple at State and Randolph. In 1899, the brothers closed this basement location and opened the DeJonghe Hotel and Restaurant in the Loop at 12 East Monroe. In those early days of Chicago dining, just a few decades after the Great Fire, standalone restaurants were not yet a "thing," and hotels were frequently where people went to dine out. Many times, the food served in these hotels was considered "gourmet," or at least much more refined than you'd expect in roadside taverns. For instance, according to Greg Borzo in "Lost Restaurants of Chicago," DeJonghe Hotel and Restaurant helped popularize escargot in Chicago, and such fancier French-type foods is what you'd expect to find in early Chicago restaurants.

In 1923, during Prohibition, the DeJonghe Hotel and Restaurant was shut down for liquor violations. The *Chicago Tribune* reported that a prohibition agent posing as a "traveling man from Boston" registered at the hotel under the name "Mr. Johnson." This undercover fed began a casual chat with Hotel Manager James T. Hickey, who introduced him to a head waiter who then allegedly sold the agent several pints of whiskey. The ensuing raid led to the seizure of thirty cases of liquor. The feds did not buy Hickey's claim that the liquor belonged to a guest who had fled the hotel and just left his thirty cases of hooch behind in lieu of paying his bill. No doubt, Hickey's defense was not helped by the fact that several months before this incident, Hickey, a hotel clerk, and three couples had been busted in the hotel on vice charges.

SHRIMP DEJONGHE IN THE 21ST CENTURY

Emil Zehr was the chef at the DeJonghe Hotel and Restaurant, and it's quite likely that he was the inventor of shrimp DeJonghe, which is now considered one of Chicago's iconic foods.

As with chicken Vesuvio, which has led to such dishes as steak Vesuvio and pork Vesuvio, there are many variations on the basic theme of shrimp in garlic and butter. It's not uncommon to see lobster or crab DeJonghe, and some variation of the traditional dish even shows up in places like Red Lobster. There's no denying it: garlic and butter complement many fruits of the sea.

At Hugo's Frog Bar and Fish House (1024 North Rush), Chef Russell Kook does a mostly traditional version of shrimp DeJonghe, "but we add Dijon mustard," says Kook, "to provide a little acidity. And you need the acidity from the mustard, wine, and lemon juice to balance the richness of the butter and the cream. The mustard also adds a savory note to the dish that our customers really like."

For the wine, says Kook, "We use a pinot gris because we want the wine flavor to be in the background, not the foreground." In the DeJonghe Hotel and Restaurant, sherry was used—at least before the place was busted.

Shrimp DeJonghe is the right dish to serve at Hugo's Frog Bar and Fish House, says Kook, "because we want to serve food that fits the surroundings. We have an old school space, and we want our food to reflect the atmosphere."

Shrimp DeJonghe, Kook tells us, is a "big favorite with customers, who appreciate the tradition, and when they're eating Shrimp DeJonghe, they're eating Chicago history."

No doubt about it: shrimp DeJonghe is old school; it's one of the rare Chicago original foods that was intended for a fine dining restaurant rather than a streetside stand or other such humble venue.

Incidentally, food historian Dr. Peter Engler brought to my attention the fact that on an existing menu from DeJonghe Hotel and Restaurant, the dish is listed as Shrimps DeJonghe, with an "s" after the word "shrimp."

WHERE TO GET SHRIMP DEJONGHE

Joe's Seafood, Prime Steak & Stone Crab
60 E. Grand Ave.
312-379-5637

Hugo's Frog Bar and Fish House
1024 N. Rush St.
312-640-0009

Italian Village
71 W. Monroe St.
312-332-7005

HOW TO PREPARE SHRIMP DEJONGHE AT HOME

When Henri de Jonghe passed away in 1961, the recipe for shrimp DeJonghe went with him. Here is a version of the original recipe that appeared in the *Chicago Tribune* in 1985; it was provided by Emil G. Zehr, the son of the man who may have invented this dish (or who prepared the first known version of shrimp DeJonghe to appear on a menu).

Ingredients

- 14 cups homemade white breadcrumbs, see step 1
- 3 cups homemade brown breadcrumbs, see step 1
- 2 pounds butter
- 1 pound margarine
- ⅓ cup chopped shallots
- 1 tablespoon Worcestershire sauce
- 3 drops liquid hot pepper sauce
- 1 cup chopped fresh garlic
- 1 cup chopped parsley
- 12 large shrimp, cooked, peeled, and cleaned

Preparation

1. Make your breadcrumbs from French or Italian bread, 3 days old. This has a great deal to do with its fine texture when finished.
2. Knead butter and margarine until soft. Add remaining ingredients except shrimp to butter mixture. Mix well in a wooden bowl. Form into sausage-like forms and place in refrigerate to set.
3. Cover bottom of casserole with ⅛-inch slices of butter mixture. Place 12 large shrimp on top of butter mixture slices. Cover shrimp with ¼-inch slices of butter mixture. Put in hot oven (375 to 400 degrees Fahrenheit) and bake until the breadcrumbs are brown, 10 to 15 minutes.

27

STEAK AND LEMONADE

Monica Eng

GRIDDLED SHAVED BEEF, ONIONS, AND PEPPERS ON A MAYO-SMEARED HOAGIE ROLL, TOPPED WITH TOMATO SLICES, LETTUCE, AND MELTED WHITE CHEESE, SERVED WITH A COLORFUL, SLUSHY DRINK

A classic Chicago steak and lemonade combo. Photo: Monica Eng

Some towns boast famous combos of wine and cheese. Doughnuts and coffee. Or beer and brats.

But on Chicago's South and West Sides, we serve up famous steak and lemonade. So famous that "Chicago style" restaurants sell the combo in towns as far away as Indianapolis, Indiana, and Louisville, Kentucky.

It's a treat that hundreds of Chicagoans scarf and sip every day, but if you mentioned it to most non–African American North Siders, you'd be treated to a blank stare. That's because steak and lemonade, like too many Chicago-invented foods, breaks down cleanly along racial and geographic lines as yet another testament to the city's longstanding segregation.

I only learned the origins of this combo a few years ago when I was commissioned to answer a question about steak and lemonade restaurants for WBEZ's Curious City show. The question came from a white listener who had passed steak and lemonade restaurants all over the city's South Side and South Suburbs for years, but never knew exactly what they served inside.

WHAT IS STEAK AND LEMONADE?

The "steak" is no sirloin or T-bone but instead a Chicagofied version of the Philly cheesesteak sandwich. Most start with griddle-cooked shaved beef, onions, and peppers on a mayo-smeared hoagie roll, topped with tomato slices, lettuce, and melted white cheese—sorry, no Cheez Whiz for us here in Chicago.

Some versions are more flavorful than others. For instance, the Philly at Baba's Famous Steak & Lemonade on 71st Street and Jeffrey uses a zesty seasoning that gives the meat a boost of heat.

Like most South Side sandwiches, the "steak" here is served with free fries whether you order them or not. And, of course, you must be ready to tell the counter staffer if you want hot sauce, mild sauce (chapter 20), or lemon pepper on them.

When you order your lemonade, don't count on some tart yellow beverage. Instead, expect a multicolored slushy-type drink, topped with your choice of blueberry, cherry, fruit punch, grape, orange, pineapple, piña colada, strawberry, or watermelon syrup. Much like the concentrates used on snow cones, these create sugary rainbows atop the lemony drink that make my teeth ache just remembering them.

Some places top the lemonade with real slices of lemon, pineapple, or strawberry to give it a touch of nature. But don't be fooled. This might be the sweetest artificially colored thing you drink all year. (Hey, I'm a health writer, too, so I can't help mentioning this stuff.) The whole icy creation is capped with a clear plastic dome lid, often associated with Asian bubble teas, and then wrapped in cling film that gets pierced by a straw when it's time to drink.

WHO CAME UP WITH THE COMBO?

I suspected early on that the creator of steak and lemonade would be an Arab American. That's because nearly every spot I visited was owned by Arab entrepreneurs—largely Palestinian, Jordanian, and Egyptian Americans. None I spoke to could pinpoint exactly why so many Arab Americans had gotten into the steak and lemonade business. They mostly conjectured that one guy started opening South Side sandwich shops (not specifically steak and lemonade joints) in the 1980s, and after he taught family and friends the business, they branched out and started their own similar places.

But which Arab American dreamed it up first? I tried to sleuth it out by visiting nearly a dozen steak and lemonade restaurants around the city and suburbs with a WBEZ intern.

Many of the places were in neighborhoods suffering from crime, poverty, disinvestment, and drug trafficking. In fact, when we arrived at our first stand on the West Side, a couple of salespeople in the parking lot assumed we were there to buy their wares.

"No thanks," I said, waving, wondering if it had been a great idea to bring an intern along. "We're just looking for steak and lemonade today."

Once inside, we ordered our food and I tried to talk to the manager through the bulletproof glass. I told him that we wanted to know about the origins of the combo. The request was met with consternation by this staffer, who wanted to be known only as "Mohammed."

"Meet me at that door over there," he said, motioning to a door leading to a storage room and kitchen. "You shouldn't stand out there for a long time. Now what are you asking about?"

I explained to him that we were there to research a story for the radio about the origin of steak and lemonade. As we chatted, one of his cooks strolled into the storage room and mentioned that he had some ideas.

"There was a guy in California doing lemonades off a shopping cart, and when he came to Chicago, he just integrated the Philly with the frozen lemonade," the cook said, asking us to only identify him as Johnny.

But his boss Mohammed shook his head and gave me a different story.

"That is not true," he said. "It comes from the Middle East."

"Really?" I asked. "Where in the Middle East?"

"Jordan," Mohammed said. "From a man called Haitham Allabadi from Jordan."

"Where can I find Haitham?" I asked.

"I don't know," Mohammed said, "but he still owns some steak and lemonade restaurants."

With this info, we thanked the staff, picked up our bag of steak sandwiches and lemonade, and headed to the car. As we sunk our teeth into the first steaks, we were impressed. The sandwich was beefy, cheesy, hefty, and filling. And the lemonade, well, I don't think I tasted much lemon, but I sure tasted the sugar. As we sipped and munched on the food, we also chewed over the conflicting theories we'd just heard.

The California and Jordan theories seemed potentially promising, but Internet and newspaper clip searches didn't turn up any popularity for Philly-like cheesesteak sandwiches paired with supersweet lemonade slushies in either of those parts of the world.

Still, the lead about this Haitham guy had a little more meat. In fact, several other staffers and owners we interviewed that week mentioned a man named Haitham as a possible founder. But several more insisted the founder was a man named Mario, whom, they said, we could find if we visited a Baba's Famous Steak and Lemonade (one of the most common names for this type of restaurant) in Joliet, about forty-five miles southwest of downtown Chicago.

So, I called the Joliet restaurant and talked to a manager named Zahir. He confirmed that the restaurant was indeed owned by a man named Mario, and that he might be able to arrange a meeting. A few days later, Zahir called to say I could meet with Mario if I drove to Joliet on an appointed date.

When the day came, I picked up Johnny Schulte and we trekked out to Joliet for the big meeting. We were surprised when we arrived at a tidy blue, yellow, and white building on Jefferson Street. It was bright, cheerful, and well lit, with no bulletproof glass in sight. Zahir greeted us heartily at the counter and disappeared into the back, saying, "I'll tell Mario you are here."

We held our breath and milled about the empty restaurant, astonished at how different it was from its less inviting city counterparts. Just then a friendly man with a mustache, jeans, and a black, button-down shirt appeared with his hand extended.

"Hello, I am Haitham Allabadi."

"Hello," I said shaking his hand. "Nice to meet you. But then who is Mario?"

"Mario is my nickname," he said, laughing. "An Italian guy gave me [it] when I was working in a kitchen in Austria."

Over the next hour he proceeded to clear up a lot of details. He explained that he was born and raised in Jordan, studied food service in college, then worked in fine dining in Europe, and finally immigrated to the United States in the 1990s. By 1998, he said, he opened his first American restaurant in Chicago's south suburbs.

"My first restaurant was in Country Club Hills," he said. "I opened this store like fast food. Not five stars, more like one star, just something for the neighborhood like Philly steak. And I make everything fresh, from scratch. I make the lemonade . . . fresh homemade lemonade from scratch too."

He said his devotion to icy lemonade came from a family recipe in Jordan, where a slushy-type of mint-flavored lemonade called limonana is famous.

"I make it like my grandfather," Allabadi said. "He's got a small store back home in my country, Jordan, and he sells lemonade—slushy lemonade with ice and different colors and flavors."

Although he calls his sandwich a Philly on the menu, he claims it's not just a wholesale copy.

"It's a little bit different," he said. "We use fresh onions, fresh mushrooms, green peppers, mozzarella, and mayonnaise, and we buy fresh every day from Turano [Bakery] which delivers at around six in the morning. And in Philadelphia, they put cheese at the top, and we don't put cheese at the top."

He said he also tweaked the sandwich in another way, inspired by Pizza Puffs.

"We also do the crispy Philly steak with tortilla bread, where we put everything inside the tortilla bread and put it in the deep fryer and it comes crispy, and we serve it with sour cream for dipping," he said. "Because I see Pizza Puff, and they use the tortilla bread, so I got the idea to do the same thing and make it crispy too."

By tortilla bread, he means a big flour tortilla.

Given the massive popularity of the steak sandwiches and the lemonade, he said he just paired them for a catchy name.

"These two were my best sellers, so I decided to market them together like dinner with a drink," he said. "It was an easy name and a simple name. We wanted people to know that we are famous for steak and lemonade, like a dinner and a drink. And 'Baba's,' which means dad in Arabic, is like going to [your] father or daddy's house."

By 2006, Allabadi trademarked the name "Baba's," and hangs the document to prove it on his wall. He opened his first Chicago Baba's at 71st and Jeffery in the South Shore neighborhood, and then several others all over the South Side and suburbs because, he says, "I could find a cheap rent."

Allabadi said his one foray to the North Side was a Baba's on Addison Street, near Wrigley Field where he opened a spot despite the higher rent. But the gamble didn't pay off.

"Did you know that they only have games there at Wrigley Field about eighty days a year?" he asked me. "And those are the only days when you do a good business. So, I closed it down."

Despite Allabadi's claim on the name Baba's Famous Steak and Lemonade, it didn't stop others from trying to capitalize on it.

"A lot of people put Super Baba, Little Baba, Great Baba and everybody wanted to steal the name," he said.

So, in 2013 he sold most of his places and kept just three in the South and West suburbs. These locations, he said, are easier for him to manage. But he is also still innovating. Allabadi said he's working on several ice cream creations using pieces of candy bars, and he's also working on a project to build the city's largest steak sandwich.

"If I do [the world's biggest steak sandwich], I think it should be covered by the Channel 7 news," he said.

In the meantime, Allabadi says he's happy that his creation has brought so much culinary joy to folks across the Midwest. But he's no longer interested in owning a huge stable of properties anymore. Instead, he said, he wants to focus on managing the few he has left and staying happy.

In recent years, he's launched a new item at his shops called Baba's "spicy burger," where he mixes bold gyros-like spices into the ground beef of a burger patty, a bit like what Greek diners were serving on spits back in the mid-1960s.

"I love my job," he said. "Anyone, he can just cook the food, but when you work with your heart you always have a great job and great food."

WHERE TO GET A STEAK AND LEMONADE

Baba's Famous Steak & Lemonade
925 W. Jefferson St.
Joliet, IL
815-722-2220

Baba's Famous Steak & Lemonade
7100 S. Michigan Ave.
773-873-0676

Baba's Famous Steak & Lemonade
3407 W. Madison St.
872-281-5522

28

SWEET STEAK SUPREME SANDWICH

Monica Eng

A KIND OF PHILLY CHEESESTEAK, WITH TOMATO SLICES, RELISH, SWEET OR HOT PEPPERS (OR BOTH), AND SWEET SAUCE

Sweet steak sandwich from Home of the Hoagy. Photo: Monica Eng

Depending on where you are in this book, you might have noticed that Chicago lays claim to A LOT of beef-based sandwiches.

Maybe it's a vestige of our stockyard history, which gave entrepreneurs access to lots of meat scraps to experiment with. Or maybe it's some unconscious rivalry with Philadelphia, to try to match its iconic cheesesteak sandwich.

Either way, the Chicago food pantheon is stuffed full of hot beefy treats sporting tasty origin stories and distinctive flavor profiles. But the one with the most colorful flavor profile, at least in my book, has to be the sweet steak supreme sandwich (aka sweet steak, steak sweet, or steak sandwich), invented by Edward Perkins Sr. on the South Side in the early 1970s. Fans of the Jim Shoe may argue otherwise, but you can read chapter 17 and decide for yourself.

WHAT IS A SWEET STEAK?

The first bite of a sweet steak—the term I've heard used most often for the sandwich—recalls an Italian beef that drove through a Big Baby (chapter 2), a bucket of mild sauce (chapter 20), and a Chicago hot dog (chapter 9) by way of Philadelphia on its way to your mouth.

So how did this combination of flavors come together? I talked to Ed Perkins II, who says his father (who passed away in 2016) got the idea sometime in the late 1960s, after he'd opened his first Taurus Flavors restaurant at 79th and Morgan in 1966. Back then the specialties at Taurus (so named for Perkins's astrological sign) were ice cream and something called the Master Dog.

"The Supreme wasn't on that original menu," the younger Perkins said. "But my dad would go to Philly all the time and hang out with his army buddy Willie Price, who had a few ice cream shops of his own.

"While he was there, he tried hoagies and Philly cheesesteaks, and he took those ideas back to Chicago. But he had to come up with a version [of the Philly] that people here in Chicago would like."

The younger Perkins said the sandwich may have been inspired by the Philly cheesesteak, but once his dad got done experimenting, "it was nothing like the original Philly."

Indeed, where a Philly cheesesteak goes savory and cheesy, this creation leans way into the world of sweet and juicy. Instead of provolone and Cheese Whiz, the Sweet Steak uses a parade of locally inspired condiments, which include:

- American cheese and grilled onions (a la Big Baby)
- Tomato slices, a steamed bun, and sweet green relish (a la Chicago hot dog)
- Sweet peppers and sometimes hot peppers (a la an Italian beef sandwich)
- Mild sauce (a la pretty much any South Side snack shop)

"Chicago is famous for mild sauce, which is kind of a sweeter version of barbecue sauce," Perkins said. "And so that's the last thing we put on the sandwich."

By combining these ingredients with griddled ribeye beef on a soft steamed steak roll, Perkins said, "We finally figured out something the Chicago taste buds would like."

Perkins Sr. dubbed it the Supreme Steak and debuted it in 1971 at Taurus Flavors, which was already famous for its hoagies.

The two sandwiches were prominently featured in a 1972 Taurus Flavors ad that ran in the *Chicago Defender*, using some catchy taglines. The hoagies were promoted as "A meal and a treat/That's all full of meat." And the supreme steaks were: "A meal in a bun/Good for everyone."

The ad listed eight Taurus Flavors locations all over the South Side and even one in Chester, Pennsylvania, presumably owned by Perkins Sr.'s friend Willie Price. Price's name was featured in a list of Perkins's seven business partners, called "the Clan" in the ad. Others on the list included Roosevelt McCarthy, who would later open another famous sweet steak restaurant.

THE RISE AND FALL OF TAURUS FLAVORS

According to the *Chicago Crusader*, there were as many as thirteen Taurus Flavors locations on the South Side at the height of the business. But Perkins II said some of those locations were not official.

"My father had a lot of people—Army buddies and whatnot—who branched off [with their own locations] without an official blessing," Perkins said. And this led to what he cryptically called "drama."

By 2001, Ed Perkins Sr. had pared his Taurus operations down to a flagship location at 85th and Stony Island in Avalon Park. In March of that year, a robbery there resulted in more drama: the murder of a well-loved manager named Queen Smith, who had been with the business for thirty years. Further investigations revealed that the assailants were former employees.

Perkins Sr. told *The Crusader* at the time that the incident didn't reflect the character of many of the people he'd employed over the years, and he wasn't going to let the tragedy run him out of the neighborhood. He didn't. Perkins Sr. continued to successfully run the business with his wife, Bernice, until his death in 2016.

In the wake of their father's death, daughter Kecia and son Ed Perkins II took over the business and watched it gain a whole new life, sparked by an article in the *Chicago Reader* by writer Ernest Wilkins.

Wilkins argued that the sweet steak belonged on Chicago "best of" lists but had been overlooked for decades by the largely white, North Side–centric food media. What followed were visits from television shows and "mainstream" food journalists including the Thrillist website, whose video on sweet steaks went viral within months.

On a good day, the restaurant was selling more than a thousand sweet steak and submarine sandwiches, according to co-owner Kecia Perkins, who spoke to the *Chicago Sun Times* in 2019.

But that was all before a new tragedy struck, that same year. A car rammed into the small Taurus Flavors building, caving in a corner of the structure. But even with the damage, demand remained strong, and the Perkinses continued to sell sandwiches out of the back door.

Within weeks, though, city inspectors shut the operation down. The Perkins siblings wrote in a blog post that their insurance couldn't cover the full cost of reconstruction, and that employees had been embezzling from them for years, even as they kept prices as low as $4.95 a sandwich.

At press time, Ed Perkins II said he was working on a plan to rebuild and launch a Taurus food truck but had no firm date.

ANOTHER SWEET STEAK THAT'S "SANCTIONED AND BLESSED"

Despite the uncertain future of the Perkins-owned Taurus, you can still find the sandwich at other South Side restaurants, including some with Taurus in the name. But Perkins II does not vouch for them. In fact, quite the contrary.

"The only one my father helped to found and helped to stay in business was his friend Roosevelt McCarthy's restaurant called Home of the Hoagy," Perkins said. "He was one of the only ones sanctioned and blessed by my father. Everyone else you see now is not sanctioned and blessed by my father. So, there is a lot of drama and a lot of legality issues that are going on right now."

In 2020, during the pandemic, Home of the Hoagy on 111th Street saw unprecedented lines for their sweet steak sandwich. On a visit, I waited with several masked customers lined up before the restaurant even opened.

"Business has been booming," said McCarthy's daughter Denise Brown, who took over the business from her late father in 2016. "Every day since the pandemic's been going on, we've been super busy. We've had tons of call-ins and walk-ins, and I can't hardly get enough help to keep up."

Brown says the special house-made mild sauce is a big part of the restaurant's success, after fifty-plus years. She says she makes her father's special mild sauce formula every day, pouring it over sweet steaks—but also drenching their fries in it as a specialty of the house.

HOW DO YOU PREPARE A SWEET STEAK?

Perkins says the sandwich starts with sliced ribeye steaks.

"We used to get these rib eyes that were like a long tube of lunch meat, and we would slice it nice and thick, and then we would take that meat and cook it on the grill," he recalled. "We'd chop the mess out of it and just pulverize the meat. It's not supposed to be ground but chopped."

Next up, grilled onions chopped into a medium dice, which Perkins says, "is the perfect consistency to mix with the meat once it's about three quarters the way cooked on the grill."

Once the onions are translucent, Perkins says it's time to whip out a steamed steak sandwich bun and some American cheese.

"You have your portion of steak on the grill—maybe about half or quarter pound—and you cover it with two slices of American cheese," he explained. "We tried a little bit of everything, and the American cheese is the one people seem to like the most. So, you melt that American cheese on top of the meat, put the steamed bun face down on top of it and flip it all over like a burger and put the other stuff on it."

That other stuff is the elder Perkins's unusual choice of condiments that have nonetheless proven a winning combination for legions of Chicago fans.

"The traditional way is two slices of tomatoes and those sweet peppers mixed in with sweet pickle and proprietary ingredients," he said. "It's basically like a relish—sweet but with a little bit of tang from the peppers and some crunch. Some people love it. Some people hate. And some people say, 'Give me extra!'"

And for the final flourish, the sandwich gets a saucy drenching that recalls Mexican tortas ahogada or wet Italian beefs, only much sweeter.

"You put that sauce on after you dress the sandwich, wrap it up and it's done," Perkins said. "That is the traditional steak supreme sandwich."

A VEGETARIAN FUTURE FOR THE STEAK SUPREME?

Despite his family's historic business in meat sandwiches, Perkins is a longtime vegetarian. It's a practice that started in high school on a bet but has continued into his forties.

As he contemplates a future for his family's business—which, at press time, he hoped to reopen—he says customers shouldn't be surprised if a vegetarian Supreme sandwich ends up on the new menu. So, will something like soy-based texturized vegetable protein (TVP) take the place of the ribeye?

"TVP is one way of going about it, but it's a little grainy," Perkins said. "There is another way using walnuts that I've tried, and it's pretty good but you have to watch out for nut allergies."

Perkins said his family may try to offer the sandwich (vegetarian or otherwise) in a pop-up capacity as they figure out how to reboot the business, "but we've got quite a hill to go up."

At press time Perkins and his sister Kecia were still trying to organize a comeback for Taurus. Stay tuned.

WHERE CAN YOU GET A SWEET STEAK SUPREME SANDWICH?

Home of the Hoagy
1316 W 111th St.
773-238-7171

Mr. Hoagie
12303 S Halsted St.
773-614-8449

Hailey's Hoagies
1055 W 63rd St.
773-424-4439

TAFFY GRAPES

David Hammond

FRESH, SEEDLESS GREEN GRAPES DIPPED IN FROSTING, SPRINKLED WITH NUTS

Taffy grapes. Photo: David Hammond

Baba's Famous Steak and Lemonade on Laramie, like many other small take-out places all over Chicago, is designed for a grab-and-go lunch, dinner, or early breakfast (the place closes at two a.m., the better to snag some stragglers from the night before). It's not a terribly inviting space: you enter a big room hung with random, time-worn posters for branded food and beverages, order through the bulletproof glass, put your money down, and receive your food from a spinning plastic carousel. The room contains no tables or chairs, and most people hustle their food back to their homes or places of employment; I ate off the hood of my car, as the key to enjoyable quick-service meals is usually to eat them as quickly as possible, while they're still warm.

At this Baba's location, I'd ordered a steak sandwich with mild sauce (chapter 20), a lemonade (of course!), and for dessert, taffy grapes.

Taffy grapes are fresh, usually seedless green grapes, dipped in frosting and sprinkled with nuts or candy. They're usually served at smaller, non-chain quick-service restaurants, and they seem to have been created specifically to serve as a dessert or a side dish at one of Chicagoland's many steak and lemonade (chapter 27) stores, as well as barbecue, fish, and chicken stands. These single-bite treats are usually sold in clear plastic clamshell containers; there seem to be a few dozen or so taffy grapes in every order. At Baba's, there's a case in front, near the cashier, with the grapes and a few other dessert selections.

Taffy grapes are handcrafted treats. Each grape must be dipped and placed in the container by hand. There is (currently) no machine that will do that work, and it's important to keep each dipped grape separate from the others so that they don't all merge together into one sweet—and difficult-to-eat—blob.

Why "taffy," especially as no taffy is involved in the creation of these treats? Probably because they're like taffy apples. Affy Tapples, marketed as "Chicago's Original Caramel Apple," have long been a local and national favorite, and like Affy Tapples, and all taffy apples, taffy grapes are dipped into a sweet coating and covered with nuts.

Grapes, it turns out, were just the beginning. A big name in Chicago taffy grapes is Nadia's Gourmet Grapes (temporarily closed as of this writing), which supplied many local restaurants and stands and experimented with other toppings, including toffee and key lime.

WHERE TO GET TAFFY GRAPES

Baba's Famous Steak and Lemonade
344 N. Laramie Ave.
773-473-0302

Harold's Chicken
312 S. Wabash Ave.
312-362-0442

The Cake Factory
4018 W. 127th St.
Alsip, IL
708-897-0872

HOW TO PREPARE TAFFY GRAPES AT HOME

Ingredients

Seedless grapes (larger grapes seem to work best)
Chocolate chips (white chocolate is frequently preferred)
Ground peanuts

Preparation

1. Wash grapes and pat dry.
2. Melt chocolate chips (you can use a microwave; check and stir after ten seconds).
3. Dip each grape into melted chocolate, then chopped nuts.
4. Place finished grapes into refrigerator to chill.

30

TAVERN-STYLE PIZZA

Monica Eng

PIZZA WITH A THIN, USUALLY CRACKER CRISP, CRUST, CUT INTO SQUARES

Thin-crust, crispy tavern-style pizza from Vito and Nicks Pizzeria. Photo: Monica Eng

For out-of-towners, the words "Chicago-style pizza" may conjure up visions of thick, buttery-edged deep dish slices or cheesy, hulking stuffed pies you must eat with a knife and fork.

These heavy styles have their place. And by that, I mean as yearly meals with Aunt Mabel after you take her to the Willis Tower (again). The rest of the year, though, most Chicagoans go for thin-crust pies, specifically thin-crust pizzas cut into squares.

And, in my book (literally), the apotheosis of this style is an impossibly thin-crusted, square-cut pizza that took off in Chicago taverns after World War II. Eschewing the greasy pliability of New York style, the caramelized edges of Detroit style, and the heft of other Chicago styles, these "slices" were less like a meal than dainty hors d'oeuvres, a bit like tomatoey, toasted cheese on a cracker.

It's a style that grew out of a desire to have a good time with pals at the bar without stopping for a full meal. A style that, for many Chicagoans, recalls birthday parties, bowling parties, and union meetings. And it's a style you can crank out quickly, cheaply, and without a lot of fuss.

So, it's no wonder that this pizza is often called "tavern style" or "party cut."

WHERE DID TAVERN-STYLE PIZZA BEGIN?

Chicago records show that pizza hit town in the early twentieth century. But, according to *Chicago Tribune* records, the city still boasted only one pizzeria as late as 1939—and that exotic spot was in Little Italy on Taylor Street.

There, the *Tribune* reported, proprietor Tom Granato cranked out pies whose crust was "similar to that [of] an English muffin," with Italian cheese, pear tomatoes, and olive oil on top. It sounds like a tasty pie, but much spongier than the pizzas that would emerge less than a decade later.

So, who made the first one?

That's a tough question, because so many places started serving tavern style pizza between 1946 and 1950, and not just in Italian neighborhoods. These places included the Home Run Inn in Lawndale, Italian Fiesta in Hyde Park, Father and Son in Logan Square, Marie's Pizza & Liquor in Albany Park, and Candlelite in Rogers Park.

Still, my bet for the very first Chicago tavern-style pie would go to Vito's Tavern at 79th and Carpenter in Auburn Gresham—before it moved to the Ashburn neighborhood on Pulaski Road in 1965, where it was renamed Vito & Nick's. That's where Nick Barraco returned to work with his parents, Vito and Mary, after serving in World War II, according to his daughter Rose George, who runs the business today.

"[While my dad] was in the service he contacted my grandmother Mary," she said. "And he asked her to try making a pizza that was thin, very thin. Then when he got home, they perfected it."

George said they introduced the perfected, crispy, square-cut pizza at the bar in 1946. It was very different from the focaccia-like slices her Sicilian grandma made at home, but ideal for snacking on with a drink.

“They were small pieces, and they were easy to eat,” George said. “People could sit around and help themselves, and they only needed napkins, they didn’t need a plate. It’s not messy.”

George was raised upstairs from Vito & Nick’s on Pulaski. She says she was so immersed in this style of pizza that she had never even heard of the term “tavern cut.”

“We just knew it as pizza, thin-crust pizza,” she says. “I heard about this term ‘tavern cut’ just a few years ago.”

Still, these cracker crust pies weren’t just served in Italian American neighborhoods. After World War II, they were adopted by the broader city—and in at least one case, at the encouragement of gas oven salespeople—as a great new profit stream, says Peter Regas of PizzaHistoryBook.Com.

“Chicago got the memo a little later than the East Coast that there was profit to be made in the tavern business by adding pizza,” Regas said. “And because Chicago didn’t have an existing pizzeria culture like New York had, which emerged organically from early Campania region bakers, they were freer to do nontraditional styles that were mainly about making money.”

Even Greek-owned bars like Marie’s Pizza & Liquors got on board the pizza wagon.

“My father George added it in the 1950s because it became this popular thing after the war,” says Nadine Marie Karavidas, who took over her family’s pizza and liquor institution in 2000. “But I think it just became part of the culture of taverns and community and food, and they all evolved together.”

Today you can still stand in front of Marie’s window and watch the pizza makers roll out the dough—rather than toss and stretch it the way they do in New York—to create the signature ultrathin crust that Karavidas also grew up seeing as just pizza.

“Truthfully,” Karavidas said, “I didn’t know there was any other style of pizza.”

I should note that not all Chicago thin-crust pizzas are as thin as those you find at places like Marie’s, Vito and Nick’s, and Pat’s Pizza in Lincoln Park. Some, like the ones I grew up with at Golden Crust in Albany Park, feature thicker, chewy crusts and more cheese. Still others fall somewhere in between.

In *The Ultimate Chicago Pizza Guide*, author Steve Dolinsky writes about how local pizza makers achieve their crispy foundation, noting that Pat’s rolls out the ultrathin discs using an industrial sheeter, covers them with paper, and leaves them to dry out in the cooler for five days. On top goes a light coat of not-too-sweet sauce circled right to the edges, a modest shower of mozzarella, and often nubbins of sausage flavored with fennel. In Chicago it’s also increasingly common to find briny and fiery giardiniera offered as a thin-crust topping.

While it might take several pieces of these ultrathin pies to fill you up, their light profile also keeps them affordable to the average family. And George said her father wanted her to keep it that way.

“I learned two important things from my father before he passed,” she said. “One, is that you are out there working for the working-class person. You want them to be able to come in on a weekly basis, if possible, with their family, and be able to afford it so you keep your prices as low as you can. And two, he said whether you have good times or bad times, you never ever vary the quality of your product. Never."

WHERE TO GET TAVERN-STYLE PIZZA

Vito's & Nick's
8433 S. Pulaski Rd.
773-735-2050

Pat's Pizza & Ristorante
2679 N. Lincoln Ave.
773-248-0168

Marie's Pizza & Liquors
4129 W. Lawrence Ave
773-725-1812

REFERENCES

AKUTAGAWA

Nagasawa, Katherine. "What happened to Chicago's Japanese Neighborhood?" WBEZ 91.5 Chicago, August 13, 2017. https://interactive.wbez.org/curiouscity/chicago-japanese-neighborhood/.

BIG BABY

Eng, Monica. "Nicky's and the Big Baby: A South Side Burger Mystery." From NPR Station WBEZ, August 5, 2019. https://www.npr.org/local/309/2019/08/05/734910183/nicky-s-and-the-big-baby-a-south-side-burger-mystery.

BONE-IN PORK CHOP SANDWICH

Bray, Matt. "Sport Pepper Guide: Heat, Flavor, Uses." PepperScale, August 28, 2021. https://www.pepperscale.com/sport-peppers/.

Chillag, Ian. "Sandwich Monday: Bone-In Pork Chop Sandwich." WNPR's The Salt: What's On Your Plate, March 16, 2015. https://www.npr.org/sections/thesalt/2015/03/16/393354031/sandwich-monday-bone-in-pork-chop-sandwich.

BREADED STEAK SANDWICH

Berg, Ted. "Chicago Has the Best Sandwich in the World and Most People Don't Even Know It." *USA Today*'s For the Win, March 3, 2015. https://ftw.usatoday.com/2015/03/ricobenes-chicago-best-sandwich-in-the-world-breaded-steak.

Komenda, Ed. "Ricobene's Breaded Steak Sandwich Turns 40, Still 'Best in the World.'" DNAInfo. July 1, 2016. https://www.dnainfo.com/chicago/20160701/bridgeport/ricobenes-breaded-steak-sandwich-turns-40-this-year/.

CHICKEN VESUVIO

"Antonius" (Anthony Buccini). "The Alleged Chicago Origins of 'Chicken Vesuvio.'" LTHForum, April 11, 2005. https://www.lthforum.com/bb/viewtopic.php?t=3416.

Wives with Knives. "Chicken Vesuvio, Chicago Style." July 21, 2011. http://www.wiveswithknives.net/2011/07/21/chicken-vesuvio-chicago-style/.

CHICAGO CORN ROLL TAMALE

Evans, Amy C. Southern Foodways Alliance. "An Introduction: Hot Tamales and the Mississippi Delta." Southern Foodways Alliance. Accessed April 11, 2022. https://www.southernfoodways.org/interview/hot-tamales-the-mississippi-delta/.

Marvar, Alexandra. "Hot on the Trail of Tamales, on a Road Trip through the Mississippi Delta." *Chicago Tribune*, February 14, 2020. https://www.chicagotribune.com/travel/ct-trav-mississippi-tamale-trail-0223-20200214-xnyhrkvkrna7dnnspoathttjlu-story.html.

CHICAGO MIX

Butler, Stephanie. "A History of Popcorn." History, December 6, 2013. https://www.history.com/news/a-history-of-popcorn.

Cretors, G. H. https://www.cretors.com/an-age-of-invention/.

Garrett Popcorn Shops. https://www.garrettpopcorn.com/garrett-popcorn/.

Morotti, Ally. "Garrett Popcorn Alleges Former Employee Stole Secret Recipes." *Chicago Tribune*, April 23, 2019. https://www.chicagotribune.com/business/ct-biz-garrett-popcorn-stolen-recipes-lawsuit-20190422-story.html.

Podmolik, Mary Ellen. "Garrett Popcorn Sued over Chicago Mix." *Chicago Tribune*, September 2, 2014. https://www.chicagotribune.com/business/chi-Garrett-popcorn-chicago-mix-lawsuit-20140902-story.html.

Snyder, Sabrina. "Chicago Mix Cheddar and Caramel Popcorn!" Recipe. Dinner Then Dessert, May 2, 2019. https://dinnerthendessert.com/chicago-mix-cheddar-caramel-popcorn/.

Vettel, Phil. "The Popcorn Report." *Chicago Tribune*, December 11, 1986.

CHICAGO-STYLE EGG ROLL

Chu, Louisa. "Why Do Egg Rolls in Chicago Taste Like Peanut Butter? And More Egg Roll Questions Answered." *Chicago Tribune*, March 2, 2018. https://www.chicagotribune.com/dining/craving/ct-food-chicago-deep-fried-peanut-butter-egg-rolls-20180302-story.html.

Kindelsperger, Nick. "Chicago's Egg Roll Boom Is Fueled by Black Restaurateurs, Who Fill the Chinese American Snack with Everything from Jerk Chicken to Italian Beef." *Chicago Tribune*, February 23, 2021. https://www.chicagotribune.com/dining/ct-food-egg-roll-jerk-chicken-dinkey-tastee-rolls-20210223-ryey7ffweffcxpcaefw6lcv72e-story.html.

CHICAGO HOT DOG

Eng, Monica. "Deconstructing the Chicago-Style Hot Dog." WBEZ Chicago, March 5, 2017. https://www.wbez.org/stories/deconstructing-the-chicago-style-hot-dog/1931cbb5-5fae-4da1-9d62-bdcfd2b86bf4.

DEEP DISH PIZZA

Better Homes and Gardens. "How to Make Deep-Dish Pizza." June 9, 2015. https://www.bhg.com/recipes/pizza/how-to-make-deep-dish-pizza/.

Chicago Tribune. "A History of Deep-Dish Pizza." February 18, 2009. https://www.chicagotribune.com/news/ct-xpm-2009-02-18-0902180056-story.html.

———. "Who Invented Deep Dish?" February 18, 2009. https://www.chicagotribune.com/news/ct-xpm-2009-02-18-0902180055-story.html.

Dolinsky, Steve. *Pizza City, USA*. Evanston, IL: Northwestern University Press, 2018.

Galloway, Paul. "A Half-Baked Story on How Deep-Dish Pizza Was Created in Chicago." *Chicago Tribune*. January 8, 1986. https://www.chicagotribune.com/news/ct-xpm-1986-01-08-8601020867-story.html.

Lou Malnati's Pizzeria. https://www.loumalnatis.com/about-the-pizza.

Uno Pizzeria and Grill. https://www.unos.com/.

Zemans, Dan. "Chicago's Deep Dish History: It All Started with Uno's." Eater Chicago, May 8, 2012. https://chicago.eater.com/2012/5/8/6589237/chicagos-deep-dish-history-it-all-started-with-unos.

FLAMING SAGANAKI

Borzo, Greg, and Doug Sohn. *Lost Restaurants of Chicago*. Charleston, SC: American Palate, 2018.

Fuller, Janet Rausa. "Opa! In Praise of Flaming Saganaki." *Chicago Magazine*, September 8, 2016. https://www.chicagomag.com/dining-drinking/September-2016/Opa-In-Praise-of-Flaming-Saganaki/.

Pridmore, Jay. "A Taste of Greektown." *Chicago Tribune*, May 10, 1991. https://www.chicagotribune.com/news/ct-xpm-1991-05-10-9102110357-story.html.

GIARDINIERA

Dalanti. https://dalanti.com/.

Kindelsperger, Nick. "How Giardiniera Crossed an Ocean to Become Chicago's Favorite Condiment." *Chicago Tribune*. May 19, 2017. https://www.chicagotribune.com/dining/craving/ct-Giardiniera-chicago-history-food-0524-story.html.

Mauro, Jeff. "Homemade Hot Giardiniera." Food Network. https://www.foodnetwork.com/recipes/jeff-mauro/homemade-hot-giardiniera-recipe-1925279.

GAM PONG CHICKEN WINGS

Haddix, Carol Mighton. "Net Gain Great Sea Is a Good Catch, Even without Fish." *Chicago Tribune*, August 30, 1995.

GYROS

Estiator. "At Parthenon, Everything's Symmetrical—Even the Menu." September 1, 2015. https://www.estiator.com/at-parthenon-everythings-symmetrical-even-the-menu/.

Loring, Kay. "Front Vies and Profiles: Table Talk." *Chicago Tribune*, June 20, 1969.

Nagrant, Michael. "Gyros at the Parthenon." Michael Nagrant: One Bite at a Time, January 20, 2014. https://www.michaelnagrant.com/reviews/gyros-parthenon.

———. "Worth a Trip: Gyros at the Parthenon." *Chicago Tribune*, January 22, 2014. https://www.chicagotribune.com/redeye/ct-red-parthenon-gyros-chicago-worth-a-trip-20140122-story.html.

Olympia Foods. "About Us." http://www.olympiagyros.com/about_us/about/.

Segal, David. "The Gyro's History Unfolds." *New York Times*, July 14, 2009. https://www.nytimes.com/2009/07/15/dining/15gyro.html.

South Florida Reporter. "The Gyro Made Its First US Appearance at a Chicago Restaurant in 1965." August 31, 2020. https://southfloridareporter.com/the-gyro-made-its-first-us-appearance-at-a-chicago-restaurant-in-1965-video.

ITALIAN BEEF SANDWICH

Al's Italian Beef. https://www.alsbeef.com/.

Buccini, Anthony F., and Michael Stern. "Italian Beef." In *The Chicago Food Encyclopedia*, edited by Carol Mighton Haddix, Bruce Kraig, and Colleen Taylor Sen. Urbana, IL: University of Illinois Press, 2017.

CBS Chicago, "Scala's Original," January 11, 2012, https://www.cbsnews.com/chicago/news/scalas-original/.

WGN Radio. "The Italian Beef Greats: Buona and Al's Tell Their Stories." Audio download. May 31, 2017. https://wgnradio.com/2017/05/31/the-italian-beef-greats-buona-als-tell-their-stories/.

MALÖRT

Jeppson's Malört. http://jeppsonsmalort.com/.

McNear, Claire. "Malört, Chicago's Celebrated, Foul-Tasting Liquor, Is Returning to Its Ancestral Home." The Ringer, February 6, 2019. https://www.theringer.com/2019/2/6/18211851/malort-chicago-liquor-comes-home-pat-gabelick-carl-jeppson-co-ch-distillery-midwest-expansion.

Sula, Mike. "Omnivorous: Shot of Malört, Hold the Grimace." *The Reader*, April 9, 2009. https://www.chicagoreader.com/chicago/shot-of-malort-hold-the-grimace/Content?oid=1098569.

MAXWELL STREET POLISH

Encyclopedia of Chicago. "Swedes." http://www.encyclopedia.chicagohistory.org/pages/1222.html.

Eng, Monica, and Charles Leroux. "The Original Maxwell Street Market—First with Its . . ." *Chicago Tribune*, October 1, 2004. https://www.chicagotribune.com/news/ct-xpm-2004-10-01-0410010367-story.html.

MILD SAUCE

Daley, Bill. "What's the Story? Answering a Reader's Questions about Mild Sauce." *Chicago Tribune*, June 24, 2017. https://www.chicagotribune.com/dining/ct-mild-sauce-hearken-food-0628-story.html.

Gibson, Campbell. Population of the 100 Largest Cities and Other Urban Places in the United States: 1790 to 1990. U.S. Bureau of the Census, June 1998. https://www.census.gov/library/working-papers/1998/demo/POP-twps0027.html.

MOTHER-IN-LAW

Bourdain, Anthony (host). "Chicago." *No Reservations*, Season 5, Episode 5. First aired on the Travel Channel, February 2, 2009.

Chiarito, Bob. "Johnny O's in Bridgeport Is Closing on Saturday, Marking the End of an Era." Block Club Chicago, September 18, 2019. https://blockclubchicago.org/2019/09/18/johnny-os-in-bridgeport-is-closing-on-saturday-marking-the-end-of-an-era/.

Southern Foodways Alliance. "Robert Steward, Owner & Tamale-Maker, Stewart's Quick Mart." https://www.southernfoodways.org/interview/chicago-connection/.

You and Me This Morning. "Fat Johnnie's Famous Red Hots: Part 1." YouTube video, July 7, 2016. https://youtu.be/GxLm669VWxE .

———. "Fat Johnnie's Famous Red Hots: Part 2." YouTube video, July 7, 2016. https://youtu.be/g3OdWIV2TyY.

PEPPER AND EGG SANDWICH

Ali, Tanveer. "Where to Get Pepper and Egg Sandwiches, a Chicago Lent Tradition." DNAInfo, February 11, 2016. https://www.dnainfo.com/chicago/20150220/little-italy/where-get-pepper-egg-sandwiches-chicago-lent-tradition-map.

Archdiocese of Chicago. Data Composite. Facts and Figures for the Year Ending 2021. https://www.archchicago.org/documents/70111/1884101/Data+Comp+2020v2.pdf/8ecc597a-cb66-45b3-adf8-0a9a6654deec.

Bauer, Kelly, and Tanveer Ali. "Chicago's Pepper and Egg Sandwiches Remain a Staple During Lent (and the Rest of the Year)." Block Club Chicago, February 26, 2020. https://blockclubchicago.org/2020/02/26/chicagos-egg-and-pepper-sandwiches-remain-a-staple-during-lent-and-the-rest-of-the-year/.

Behymer, Jim. "Fridays in Lent: The Pepper and Egg Sandwich." Sandwich Tribunal, March 23, 2018. https://www.sandwichtribunal.com/2018/03/fridays-in-lent-the-pepper-and-egg-sandwich/.

Cseke, Bianca. "Pepper & Egg Sandwiches for Lent—Our Map Will Help You Find Some of the Best in the Area." *Chicago Sun-Times*, March 2, 2020. https://chicago.suntimes.com/taste/2020/3/2/21158165/pepper-egg-sandwich-map-lent-easter-chicago-restaurants.

Kindelsperger, Nick. "Pepper and Egg Sandwich Recipe." Serious Eats, June 7, 2019. https://www.seriouseats.com/recipes/2013/10/pepper-and-egg-sandwich-recipe.html.

PIZZA PUFF

Schnitzler, Nicole. "Deep Dish: 107 Years of Chicago Pizza History." *Chicago Tribune*, September 16, 2016. https://www.chicagotribune.com/dining/ct-graphics-chicago-pizza-history-htmlstory.html.

RAINBOW CONE

Koeske, Zoe. "Original Rainbow Cone Gets a View: Iconic Beverly Ice Cream Parlor Opens Kiosk at Navy Pier." *Chicago Tribune*, June 16, 2016. https://www.chicagotribune.com/suburbs/daily-southtown/ct-sta-rainbow-cone-st-0614-20160616-story.html.

RIB TIPS

Goldwyn, Meathead. "History of Chicago BBQ." Illinois BBQ Alliance. Accessed April 11, 2022. http://ibbqa.org/members/membersonly/historyofchicagobbq.html.

Freeman, Sarah. "What Is Chicago-Style Barbecue, Anyway?" Eater Chicago, June 15, 2016. https://chicago.eater.com/2016/6/15/11923078/chicago-style-barbecue-history.

Uncle John's Barbecue. https://www.unclejohnsbarbecue.com/.

SHRIMP DEJONGHE

Borzo, Greg, and Doug Sohn. *Lost Restaurants of Chicago*. Charleston, SC: American Palate, 2018.

Camp, Paul A., and Jeanmarie Brownson. "The Heavenly Recipe That Helped Make Henri de Jonghe Immortal." *Chicago Tribune*, January 27, 1985. https://www.chicagotribune.com/news/ct-xpm-1985-01-27-8501060043-story.html.

Chicago Tribune. "Shrimp De Jonghe, Or Is It De Zehr?" February 21, 1985. https://www.chicagotribune.com/news/ct-xpm-1985-01-27-8501060043-story.html.

Haddix, Carol Mighton. "Shrimp DeJonghe." In *The Chicago Food Encyclopedia*, edited by Carol Mighton Haddix, Bruce Kraig, and Colleen Taylor Sen. Urbana, IL: University of Illinois Press, 2017.

SWEET STEAK SUPREME SANDWICH

Chu, Louisa. "A Video of South Side Sandwich Has Over 6 Million Views. What Makes It So Special?" *Chicago Tribune*, August 13, 2018. https://www.chicagotribune.com/dining/craving/ct-food-sweet-steak-sandwich-taurus-flavors-0822-story.html.

Hendrickson, Matthew. "City Closes Beloved Sandwich Shop Taurus Flavors after Car Crashed into It." *Chicago Sun-Times*, September 8, 2019. https://chicago.suntimes.com/metro-state/2019/9/8/20853518/taurus-flavors-hoagie-shop-avalon-park-crash.

Palmer, J. Coyden. "Owner of Taurus Flavors Edward Perkins Passes Away at 79." *Chicago Crusader*, December 15, 2016.https://chicagocrusader.com/local-news/owner-taurus-flavors-edward-perkins-passes-away-79/.

TAFFY GRAPES

Jackson, Cheryl V. "Taffy Grapes: South Side Treats that Sell Out Daily Are Spreading across Chicago." *Chicago Tribune*, June 28, 2017. https://www.chicagotribune.com/dining/ct-taffy-grapes-south-side-treat-food-0628-20170627-story.html.

Pomranz, Mike. "Are 'Taffy Grapes' the Fidget Spinners of the Food World?" *Food and Wine*, June 30, 2017. https://www.foodandwine.com/news/taffy-grapes-chicago.

TAVERN-STYLE PIZZA

Fuller, Janet Rausa. "Chicago's 10 Oldest Pizzerias Are Full of Delicious Secrets." DNAInfo. https://www.dnainfo.com/chicago/20160329/downtown/chicagos-10-oldest-pizzerias-thrive-by-not-giving-up-any-secrets/.

Schnitzler, Nicole. "Deep Dish: 107 Years of Chicago Pizza History." *Chicago Tribune*, September 16, 2016. https://www.chicagotribune.com/dining/ct-graphics-chicago-pizza-history-htmlstory.html.

Provines, June. "Front Views and Profiles: Italian Pizzeria." *Chicago Daily Tribune*, Oct 17, 1939.

Eng, Monica. "Vito & Nick's Pizzeria, Home to Chicago's Famous Tavern Crust, Celebrates 100 Years." NPR, August 13, 2020. https://www.npr.org/local/309/2020/08/13/902132298/vito-nick-s-pizzeria-home-to-chicago-s-famous-tavern-crust-celebrates-100-years. (Mary Barraco is credited with developing the tavern-style pizza.)

Ebert, Roger. "Ebert Gets to the Crust of the Matter." May 21, 1995. https://www.rogerebert.com/roger-ebert/ebert-gets-to-the-crust-of-the-matter.

MONICA ENG is a mother of two and a lifelong Chicagoan. She has worked as a reporter at the *Chicago Sun-Times*, the *Chicago Tribune*, WBEZ, and Axios Chicago for nearly four decades. Her food writing at the *Chicago Tribune* was nominated five times for the James Beard Award, and her food stories have appeared in *Gourmet*, *Bon Appetit*, and the *Washington Post*. Monica currently serves up daily dispatches for Axios Chicago, while co-hosting the Chewing Podcast with Louisa Chu and finishing a historical novel about her family's Chinese restaurant empire.

DAVID HAMMOND, born in Chicago, is a father of three, a former college English professor, and corporate communications consultant. He has written food reviews for the *Chicago Reader*, as well as the Food Detective column for the *Chicago Sun-Times*; he is a co-founder of LTHForum.com, the Chicago culinary chat site, and he has produced and hosted the Sound Bites series on Chicago Public Radio. He is currently Dining & Drinking Editor at *Newcity Chicago*, and a regular contributor to Oak Park's *Wednesday Journal* and many other local and national publications.

The University of Illinois Press
is a founding member of the
Association of University Presses.

Text designed by Jennifer S. Fisher
Composed in 7.5/11 Caecilia LT Std
with CA Negroni and Faito display
by Jennifer S. Fisher
at the University of Illinois Press
Manufactured by Versa Press, Inc.

University of Illinois Press
1325 South Oak Street
Champaign, IL 61820-6903
www.press.uillinois.edu